PRAISE FOR RAYMOND SOKOLOV's *Steal the Menu*

"Sokolov is very good company. . . . His writing is witty and engaging, but what sets this book apart is its appreciativeness: food is food for thought." —Naomi Duguid, author of
Burma: Rivers of Flavor

"*Steal the Menu* gets you a tableside seat everywhere from Tennessee barbeque pits to French haute cuisine temples."
—*Entertainment Weekly*

"A lively insider's account of goings-on in the American food scene over the last forty years. And who better to tell this story than Raymond Sokolov, one of America's best food writers? . . . By turns authoritative and funny, deeply informed and irreverent. . . . A feast for the senses as well as the mind."
—Darra Goldstein, founding editor,
Gastronomica: The Journal of Food and Culture

"Delightful." —*The Free Lance-Star* (Fredericksburg, VA)

"Anyone even remotely interested in American food is aware that the last half century of gastronomy has provided thrills, chills and exciting new sustenance, and Raymond Sokolov tells us all about it." —*The Buffalo News*

"Engaging. . . . Reading [Sokolov's *Steal the Menu*] is like being driven in an old, comfortable roadster, top down, evening falling, balmy, him in houndstooth and brogues, pontificating, but with the promise—because Sokolov always does his homework—of something really good to eat just down the road."
—*The Christian Science Monitor*

"An indispensable book for anyone and everyone who takes cooking seriously."   —Jason Epstein, author of *Eating*

"Like having dinner with one's wittiest, most erudite and charming friend, someone who knows everything worth knowing about food, its history and culture, about chefs and restaurants, about how our cuisine and our kitchens have changed over forty years—and about how to tell an authentic key lime pie from an imitation. Bon appétit!"   —Francine Prose

"Sokolov invites readers to join him around the table and to share the many repasts he's consumed, skewered, and roasted over the past forty years as a food critic. . . . Captivating and humorous, [this] inviting memoir joins the ranks of Ruth Reichl's and Judith Jones's elegant recollections of a life lived at table."
            —*Publishers Weekly* (starred review)

"A zesty stew, a chronicle of movements in cuisine across the decades and oceans. As an entertainment, *Steal the Menu* rates a full complement of stars."
            —Joseph Lelyveld, author of *Great Soul*

"Stylish, sometimes provocative, always informative, with a balanced perspective on the tumultuous changes at the table we've all lived through."
            —Dr. Andrew Weil, coauthor of *The Healthy Kitchen*

"A knowledgeable look at the transformation of fine dining over the past half century, viewed through the prism of the author's personal history. . . . Refreshingly different." —*Kirkus Reviews*

Raymond Sokolov

Steal the Menu

Raymond Sokolov ate his first meal in Detroit in
1941 and dined with tenacious curiosity in France as
a correspondent for *Newsweek*. He went on to sustain
himself writing about food at *The New York Times*
and *Natural History* magazine, and, most recently, by
covering restaurants worldwide for *The Wall Street
Journal*. He is the author of *The Saucier's Apprentice*,
the novel *Native Intelligence*, and a biography of A. J.
Liebling, *Wayward Reporter*. He lives in New York's
Hudson Valley.

ALSO BY RAYMOND SOKOLOV

A Canon of Vegetables:
101 Classic Recipes

The Cook's Canon:
101 Classic Recipes Everyone Should Know

With the Grain

The Jewish-American Kitchen

Why We Eat What We Eat

How to Cook

Wayward Reporter

Fading Feast

Native Intelligence

The Saucier's Apprentice

Great Recipes from The New York Times

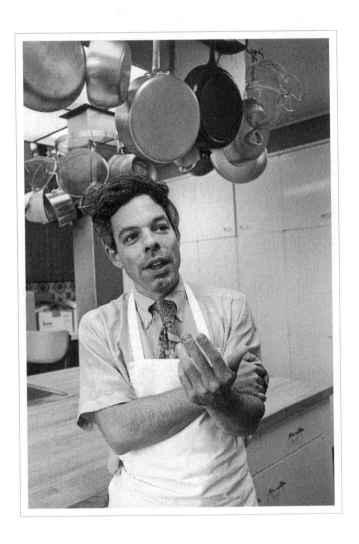

Steal the Menu

A MEMOIR OF
FORTY YEARS
IN FOOD

Raymond Sokolov

VINTAGE BOOKS
A Division of Random House LLC
New York

The Library of Congress has cataloged the Knopf edition as follows:
Sokolov, Raymond A.
Steal the menu : a memoir of forty years in food / by Raymond Sokolov.—First edition.
pages cm.
Includes index.
1. Sokolov, Raymond A. 2. Cooks—United States—Biography.
3. Food writing. 4. Cooking, American. I. Title.
TX649.S57S65 2013 641.5092—dc23 [B] 2012044156

Vintage Trade Paperback ISBN: 978-0-307-94635-5
eBook ISBN: 978-0-307-96247-8

www.vintagebooks.com

Author photograph © Stephen Shore
Book design by Cassandra J. Pappas

For Johanna

Contents

Steal the Menu

Amuse-Bouche

"There's too much bay leaf in this soup," said Craig Claiborne, after sloshing the tomato-pea *purée mongole* around in his mouth. He and I and Charlotte Curtis, his boss, were having lunch in the cafeteria of the *New York Times* in the spring of 1971. Craig was retiring as food editor of the *Times* after fourteen years in the job. He was a self-made legend, trained as a chef and a reporter, who had transformed the newspaper's food department from a sleepy recipe mill into a broad and lively forum for glamorous profiles of chefs, reports on the city's ethnic cooks and reviews of New York restaurants. He thought he could privatize his celebrity and his omnivorous yet rigorous approach to food with a personal newsletter about restaurants and cooking. Charlotte, in a huge gamble, had hired me as his successor.

Curtis was another *Times* legend. A midwestern socialite with hair pulled back tight, she was a newsroom lifer. As women's news editor, in charge of a big and increasingly important area, she presided over the Family/Style page, where Craig's articles appeared. In her earlier *Times* career, as a society reporter, Charlotte had made readers smile with her tart flair for skewering vapid brides in her coverage of big-time weddings.

In an account of a shower for Julie Nixon prior to her marriage to David Eisenhower, Charlotte wrote, "And by afternoon's end, [Richard Nixon's younger daughter] was knee-deep in such essentials as sachets made to look like roses, scented candles, bookends and a silver engraving of her wedding invitation." The article skipped on insouciantly to a dinner-dance at the Waldorf Towers, where President Nixon joined Julie's young pals during a break from appointing cabinet secretaries. In four impeccably factual words about the presidential drop-in, Charlotte summarized the man himself: "He did not dance."

Craig, a gentlemanly native of Sunflower, Mississippi, had parlayed a degree in journalism from the University of Missouri and a diploma from a Swiss hotel school into the *Times* food job. His shrewd instincts for capitalizing on the new craze for food had transformed a sleepy, creaky woman's-page service feature into a glamorous star turn. It had also made him rich.

Back in 1960, when Craig had been food editor for only three years and *Times* management hadn't yet realized they'd spawned a *monstre sacré* in their food department, Craig requested permission to use the *Times* name and its sacrosanct Times logo for a cookbook to be entitled *The New York Times Cookbook*. According to legend, barely concealing a smirk, the paper's managing editor, Turner Catledge, waved the young man on—to delirious success.

Harper & Row had never stopped selling the book.

How much did Craig owe to the *Times* connection? I inclined to the cynical, if unprovable, view that without that logo and the official-sounding title, the book would not have gone anywhere merely on the strength of the relatively unknown author's name.*

---

* Indeed, to be frank, it was in the back of my mind to publish my own sequel to *The New York Times Cookbook*, with recipes I would bring to the paper. Or, as I soon learned,

By 1971, however, Craig had made a name for himself, at least among *Times* readers. He believed he could sail on happily without the *Times* and without sweating deadlines for four features every week. He could, he believed, continue his reign as New York's food czar in independent splendor. I took him to think that some lesser being would man the food-beat treadmill at the paper, reinforcing by his jejune mediocrity the myth of the matchless Craig.

And I was going to be that man.

In Craig's world, I was indeed a nobody. I'd never taken a cooking class, published a restaurant review or written a recipe. My credentials as a cultural journalist at *Newsweek*, where I was currently working, were honorable; not too long before I'd been on the short list to become the *Times*' lead book critic. But in the kitchen, I was a cipher. However, the ego of a child prodigy had kept me from seeing that I had no business at this table, in this cafeteria, with Craig Claiborne and Charlotte Curtis.

When Craig commented on the bay leaf in the *purée mongole*, I sneered inwardly. Couldn't he see how ridiculous it was to play the gourmet with an old-fashioned soup made in a corporate cafeteria kitchen? This was the place the *New Yorker*'s resident gastronome and press critic, A. J. Liebling, had mocked in a jab he once took at newspaper editors:

---

maybe I wouldn't have to spend years accumulating enough material for a book of my own. After I was able to look at the food-department ledgers that contained paste-ups of *Times* recipes going back decades before Claiborne had arrived, I saw how he had produced his book so soon after he became food editor.

Once he had his contract, Claiborne had apparently flipped through those ledgers, much of whose contents had been produced by his predecessors, and hastily checked the ones he liked with a thick No. 1 pencil before handing the ledgers over to a typist. This process would explain why the cookbook he produced has multiple versions of the same recipes—brandied tutti-frutti I and brandied tutti-frutti II, cold tomato soups I and II, mousses au chocolat I and II. Craig seemed to have forgotten he'd already put a check mark beside the first versions by the time he put checks by the second ones in ledgers from later years, but the editorial process at Harper & Row inevitably put them side by side and no one bothered to choose between them before the draft went to press.

. . . they come to newspapers like monks to cloisters or worms to apples. They are the dedicated. All of them are fated to be editors except the ones that get killed off by the lunches they eat at their desks until even the most drastic purgatives lose all effect upon them. The survivors of gastric disorders rise to minor executive jobs and then major ones, and the reign of these nonwriters makes our newspapers read like the food in *The New York Times* cafeteria tastes.

Did Craig think he'd give me a bad moment with his bay leaf gambit? Actually, I now think he was just surrendering to the reflex of commenting expertly about the food in front of him, just as he had in print for seven hundred Fridays. In any case, I knew that my palate couldn't have detected a heavy hand with bay leaf in that soup. And from now on I'd be expected to uncover serious chefs' omissions and commissions, to unmask them with confidence for an audience of demanding *Times* readers. If I had truly understood the meaning of this moment, it would have been that the prospect of all the meals I would consume for the *Times*—and the need to judge them—ought to have made me cut and run.

Instead, I asked Craig if he had any advice for me as a restaurant critic.

"Steal the menu," he said. "If you ask for it, they might give it to you or they might not. But if they don't, they'll be watching you and counting them when they take them away after you've ordered. So just put it in your lap, fold it up and slip it in your pocket. You might look like you're playing with yourself under there, but no waiter is going to bother you about that."

FORTY TUMULTUOUS YEARS in the world of food have passed since that lunch at the *Times*. The other day, I thought about the changes that had revolutionized and mostly improved what we can eat now at a bistro in Manhattan across from Lincoln Center called Bar Boulud.

No one could have imagined such a spot in the placid, static, mediocre dining world of 1971. Today, we take for granted a lineup of star chefs transmuting remarkable ingredients of the highest quality into novel dishes tangentially based on the dusty classics still in faded vogue when I covered New York restaurants for the *Times*. The closest America had to a TV top chef then was Julia Child performing *coq au vin* for an audience of home cooks eager to learn to make French dishes correctly. Julia's breezy, offhand manner enticed a generation away from the stultifying distortions of the home economists who ruled at most food magazines and newspaper food pages. She was also an authentic counterforce to "continental" menus pushing fancy food with no roots anywhere except possibly American hotel kitchens, flaming steak Diane and butter-oozing veal *francese*.

Forty years later, after the ancien régime in French cuisines gave way to the nouvelle cuisine of Michel Guérard, the Troisgros brothers and Paul Bocuse, and then passed its baton to a global network of master chefs, Daniel Boulud, a classically trained French pro, presides with star quality over a small empire of inventive restaurants that bear his name. The meal I ate in 2010 at his informal Bar Boulud was a model of a modern meal, of a cosmopolitan way of eating that has spread from Paris all across America, and to Lima and Manila as well.

That lunch at Bar Boulud was typical of the radical sophistication of our bustling creative food scene, with its nonclassic ingredients (arugula), lighthearted plating (*boudin noir*—blood sausage—sculpted into three squat cones), the non-French wait-staff of both sexes, wine from what General de Gaulle might have called "all azimuths."* And yet each of these radical departures can be traced to changes in French restaurant kitchens that radiated around the world and have now been absorbed by "native" cooks from Iceland to Patagonia.

You could even say that Boulud has returned to his roots in a way that would have been impossible in the naive New York of 1971. When I did a feature with a New York–based French *charcutier* for the *New York Times* forty years ago, the man had been forced to abandon his trade, because New York couldn't support even one artisanal sausage maker. He showed me how to make a batch of blood pudding (with veal blood, because pork blood couldn't be sold legally in New York), an everyday favorite in France that was then unobtainable in New York. So the boudin casually reinvented at Bar Boulud in 2010 was not only a sign of postmodern creativity but also an example of the spread of authentic culinary practices from the French center to formerly unsophisticated peripheries like New York.

My personal intersection with this historical arc has not been casual. I was in the middle of various revolutions in food, recording them as a journalist, participating in them as a cook and eater. I had a front seat for all the action: the *nouvellisation* of French and then other cuisines; the role of television, starting with Julia Child on PBS and exploding into the era of the "top" chef; the emergence of the foodie, educated by cheap jet travel and ever-more-reliable cookbooks; the globalization of food ideas (fusion) and ingredients; the rise of politically correct notions of proper nutrition and ecologically sensitive food production and transport.

My life in food encompassed all of these developments, with a

---

* De Gaulle promoted France's nuclear capability as a striking force (*force de frappe*) that could defend French sovereignty anywhere (*tous azimuts*).

privileged three years of residence abroad, and very extensive gastronomic travel from 2006 to 2010, while I was writing a biweekly restaurant column for the *Wall Street Journal*.

So, in this memoir, I'll be filtering the unprecedentedly fast-moving history of food since World War II through my direct encounters with it. However, I cannot and would not want to claim to have been a primary actor in the making of these events and trends. I was there, and I ate what was put in front of me.

One

First Bites

I was born on the eve of war and Holocaust on August 1, 1941, at Harper Hospital in Detroit. By family legend, I began eating immediately and with prophetic zest. The exact content of that first meal is unrecorded, but I am sure it didn't come directly from Mom. She, like other advanced women of her time, believed that science offered a nutritionally superior and more hygienic way to feed her baby than she could herself.

Powdered "formula," dissolved in water and delivered in sterilized bottles with rubber nipples, replaced the mammalian teat in millions of American households of that era. Of course, many mothers today still choose to trade the intimate mess and exposure of nursing for the technoid ritual of preparing and delivering formula to their infants: mixing, washing and sterilizing bottles, flicking the heated "milk" on their wrists to check that it isn't too hot, remembering not to tilt the bottle too high for fear of drowning the child as he feeds, hunting for a new formula when Beloved Nipper refuses the one you started him out with.

I was not that balky kid. I never refused a bottle. Far from it. Not long after we returned home to our bastard Tudor house in the comfy Russell Woods neighborhood, I was sucking down three bottles at a feeding. At a year old, I weighed thirty pounds, and Geneva, the jovial black nanny, couldn't force my galoshes over my chubby ankles.

Did this gorging cause the allergies that afflicted me as a toddler? Childhood asthma, sensitivity to eggs, sulfa drugs, feathers, dust—they all vanished once I began eating solid food in saner amounts. By the time I turned four, my weight had become normal for my age and height, but who can say if, fourteen years later, some molecular ghost of those bottled banquets lurking in my blood didn't touch off the nearly fatal reaction I suffered from a wasp sting at an outdoor mixer at Brandeis University in the late summer of 1959. A wasp at Brandeis.

Tempting as it is to blame Mother for that (and so much else), the lusty appetite was all mine, a spontaneous urge as normal to me as a cry or a burp. She merely enabled it. Looking back on my writing career, I can't help thinking that I was born hungry and unusually interested in what I put in my mouth. Nonetheless, my family life stood behind that natural inclination.

When my paternal grandfather, Barney Sokolov, arrived in Philadelphia around 1910 from Kremenchug, a dreary industrial hub on the banks of the Dnieper in what is now Ukraine, he enrolled in an engineering program at Temple University, hoping to leave behind the life he'd known as a farmhand and the training he'd had as a bookbinder in Europe. But marriage and fatherhood came quickly. My father was born in 1912. Then news of a better life in the American West led Barney away from a technical career in Philadelphia and back to the land.

Already in 1911, another immigrant Jew, Benjamin Lipschitz, who called himself Ben Brown, had begun leading some 130 other Yiddish-speaking, socialist immigrants to the state of Utah, where they formed a Zionist agricultural commune on Homestead Act land outside the barren town of Gunnison. The Clarion Colony never overcame the triple jinx of poor soil, insufficient water and undercapitalization.* But in our family, it was remembered as a heroic adventure. Baby carriages were threatened by coyotes. Even hardy shtetl products like my grandmother were unprepared for the comfortless life, despite the cordial welcome and advice they got from Mormon neighbors.

I was also unprepared for the bleakness of Gunnison, when I managed to piggyback it onto a working trip for *Travel + Leisure* magazine. I drove through town on a great-circle tour of the mountain time zone in the 1970s, that paradisiacal era when you could get off a flight at some midpoint and continue on later, for the same fare as an uninterrupted transcontinental nonstop. As a freelance writer, I maximized my work possibilities and my private travel interests by cannibalizing a *Travel + Leisure* ticket to California, issued to me as part of an assignment for an article on fish restaurants around the country, into two segments with a stopover in Salt Lake City. I paid local rates for a Hertz car, which I then drove south through Gunnison to Death Valley, continuing on to Mount Whitney, Reno, Pyramid Lake (Nevada) and back to Salt Lake for the flight to San Francisco. Along the way, I climbed Mount Whitney and baked a cake at the summit for a *Natural History* column on high-altitude baking (the batter boiled in my camper's oven but did subside into an edible cake, which I, too nauseated from *soroche*, fed to an astonished hiker, who later nominated me, unsuccessfully, for a Guinness title as world's highest baker) and did research for my biography of A. J. Liebling, *Wayward Reporter,* at Pyramid Lake, where Liebling had reported on the evils of aerial hunting of wild mustangs. I also spent a lurid, sleepless night at an isolated motel on a lonely stretch of Interstate

---

* See Robert Alan Goldberg, *Back to the Soil: The Jewish Farmers of Clarion, Utah, and Their World* (University of Utah Press, 1986), pp. 67–68.

80 east of Winnemucca, kept awake by the angry shouts and then the ecstatic squeals of the couple in the next room.

My stop in Gunnison, Utah, had not been much pleasanter. The small town's principal landmark was a prison. As I ate a toasted cheese sandwich at a lunch counter, next to a tobacco-chewing fellow in snakeskin boots, I tried to imagine my grandfather struggling to make a go of it there.

Little had changed from the bleakness the first arrivals had seen in 1911, as Goldberg noted:

> As Ben Brown steered the wagon westward out of town, the colonists strained to see their land. . . . Although lacking in farm experience, Barney Silverman became concerned. The land sloped steeply, resembling the sides of a "large saucer." The "raw earth," as Isaac Friedlander described it, was bare of trees and covered with sagebrush, shadscale, and tall, thin grasses. Large patches of ground were devoid of any vegetation. . . . The site of the base camp was a particularly dubious place to begin cultivation. Yet, this determination was out of the Jews' control. The stage of canal construction had dictated the initial area of farming in the southern part of the colony on some of the worst land in the tract. Silverman also noticed that no well had been dug for water.

After five wretched winters, Clarion went under. Ben Brown stayed in Utah and prospered in the wholesale egg distribution business, the capitalist opposite of everything he and the Clarion Colony had once stood for. My hapless family, now including my uncle Eugene Victor Debs Sokolov, born in Utah in 1913, the year after the socialist E. V. Debs ran for president for the fourth time, decamped to that Kremenchug in Michigan, Detroit, where we had a wealthy second cousin.

Her welcome was a hollow one. She died soon of diabetes, leaving Grandpa Barney to improvise a living on the margins of the Detroit food economy. By the time I got to know him, in the early 1950s, he was operating an old-fashioned fish market— smoked whitefish, herring in barrels—on Michigan Avenue not far from the city's skid row. At one point, he had banged together coops in his backyard, raised chickens and sold them to neighbors during a butchers' strike. Even after he had his own shop, he kept his hand in as an agriculturalist with a little home vegetable garden that brought him his only worldly fame. In 1950, the gardening page of the *Detroit News* extolled the pumpkin he'd coaxed to grow up a post. When my sister and I were taken to Grandpa's house on our weekly Sunday visit, I ran eagerly out to the garden to see this wondrous climbing cucurbit. It was very small and wrinkled.

The fish market was equally uninspiring. And it came to a tragicomic end. Grandma Mary inherited the building and, guided by my father, rented it out, first as a doctor's office, then as a bookstore. Or so everybody thought. Yes, the tenants did sell books, but naughty ones, and there were girls upstairs. Police eventually raided the place, and Grandma Mary, a sheltered homebody, barely Anglophone, was cited for running a cathouse.

She, too, built a life around food, chopping carp for gefilte fish, preserving Kirby pickles with copious amounts of garlic and dill in Mason jars. We would carry home bushel baskets of them every fall, and kept them in the rec room, slightly embarrassed in our half-assimilated way, by this mark of *jener Welt*, the old country no one ever mentioned.

Although my father's first language had been Yiddish, which he relearned in after-school classes, the world of his grandparents meant little more to Daddy than it did to me. He did, however, join a Jewish congregation (very reformed) just before I was born, and volunteered for the Public Health Service after Pearl Harbor (the army turned him down because of a transient heart condition) to take a stand as a Jew against Hitler. And who would argue that for a young doctor to interrupt his career in order to teach other military doctors how to treat venereal disease with the revolutionary new wonder drug penicillin was not a selfless and effective contribution to the war effort? He and my miserable mother spent three nomadic years in a catch-as-catch-can life around army bases, fearful they'd be snubbed in allegedly anti-Semitic officers' clubs, and actually were snubbed by locals in South Carolina and Texas who had had their fill of strangers on their way to war theaters in Europe and the Pacific.

In our family mythology, these were hard times, a descent into lumpenproletarian scarcity. Mother never stopped wincing over the unpasteurized Grade D milk she had seen on supermarket shelves in El Paso, home to Fort Bliss, or retelling the horror story of the Chicano boy who tried to get me to go shoot rabbits. I was three by then, and I had heard the noise of revelry by night on V-E Day in Columbia, South Carolina, not long after my neurasthenic mother had blithely chopped off the head of a chicken she'd been raising in the yard. As I watched it run around spattering blood on the bare dirt, I had no way of appreciating the spectacle as a reenactment of Grandpa Barney's poultry caper in Detroit twenty years before.

What did I think about that chicken, my first exposure to meat production? I wish I could say that this barnyard violence troubled my soul ever after and fattened the wallets of therapists. Not so; nor have I shrunk from offing rabbits and geese when the necessity presented itself.

Mother did not continue her career as a home butcher after we left Columbia. But she did bring back one exotic culinary habit from the war. Chili.

The same Mexicans who terrified her with their low-class

Thumper bagging and unpasteurized milk also fed themselves with delicious Mexican food that she and Daddy learned to love.

How did my timorous parents, who were tenderfoots par excellence, unable even to find the Chinese laundry at Fort Bliss, end up adopting a lip-stinging Rio Grande chili as their signature family dish? No, they did not attend the annual Original Terlingua International Championship Chili Cookoff in a Texas ghost town. Instead, my parents learned about Mexican food because of gonorrhea. The leading nightclub operator in Juárez, the lively town across the border, via the bridge over the Rio Grande, heard that a doctor at Fort Bliss had a miracle drug that could cure his case of the clap. He called for an appointment, and Daddy explained that the drug was in short supply and he couldn't treat him. Even U.S. civilians couldn't normally get it, only military personnel and their "contacts." So unless this Mexican had had sex with a WAC, or perhaps a GI, and could prove it, Daddy wasn't authorized to treat him.

Horacio Gutiérrez, as I will call him, had not become the leading figure in the raffish nightlife scene of wartime Juárez by accepting refusals from low-level bureaucrats, even if they were captains in the U.S. Public Health Service. He made another phone call, this time to someone at Fort Bliss who outranked my dad, and ordered him to treat Señor Gutiérrez.

He did so quite happily and cured him. From then on, all three of us Sokolovs were *personae gratissimae* at Señor Gutiérrez's club. All of Juárez was officially off-limits to U.S. servicemen, but my father's rank was high enough to get him past the MPs at the border checkpoint. So we went often, and ate and drank on the house, developing a taste for the free food on offer in unrationed Mexico. I wore my tailor-made captain's uniform and acquired a little serape and a tiny guitar, so that I could sit in with the Mexican "magicians" when they played "Cielito Lindo" and "Amapola." It was also the beginning of my career as a student of ethnic food and as a restaurant-world insider.

My father would have shuddered at the thought that he was preparing me for a life as a gourmet. He had no respect for friends of his who cooked as a hobby or made a big fuss about fancy food. Without exactly calling a gastronomically avid friend of his a homosexual, he made it clear to me that the meal he'd just eaten at the man's house gave him doubts about the state of his host's masculinity. Certainly, the fellow was wasting his time on an unserious obsession.

But then my father, a hilarious comic when the mood came upon him, felt compelled to dismiss large areas of life as "unserious," or "making no difference in the world." His standards for seriousness were high and self-undermining. Although he was a first-rate and successful internist, he let me know from my earliest youth that he hated the practice of medicine, considered it drudgery. The intellectual quality of routine patient care was tediously low. And he retired at the first opportunity, at fifty-eight, after twin retinal detachments brought him financial independence through disability insurance. Certainly, he never gave me a word of encouragement to follow in his footsteps as a doctor. But then he never gave me a word of advice about anything important.

When I announced that I was going to major in classics at Harvard, he opined that classicists didn't make anything happen. But that was as far as he went, never offering any real opposition to the plan or even mentioning the subject thereafter.

Similarly, when I came home senior year with the news that I was intending to marry a non-Jewish woman, his reaction was one of indifference. Mother insisted that I make a special trip to see our rabbi for the first time in eight years, to tell him I was intending to marry a Christian. Dr. Richard C. Hertz of Temple Beth El tried to talk me out of the marriage. I would regret standing apart from mainstream Jewish life, he said. His trump card was that he wouldn't officiate at the ceremony.

I had the presence of mind to point out that no one had asked him.

My father never returned to that subject, either. It would have been hypocritical for him if he had, since his background and personal convictions were irreligious, despite his nominal membership at Beth El. We did not observe the Sabbath or keep a kosher home. Neither did either set of my grandparents, although Barney and Mary Sokolov had retained a bemused nostalgia for the Orthodox practices of their European childhoods. When I was five or six, we went to their house for the only Passover seder ever celebrated in a home by our family in Detroit.

It was conducted with complete fidelity to tradition. Adult men reclined at the table on pillows and washed their hands when the Haggadah commanded them to. An older cousin asked the four questions in Hebrew, English and Yiddish.

But on all other days except that one, Jewish dietary rules were ignored, even if traditional Jewish dishes from the shtetl found a place on the table. From this liberated platform, my father and his classy if unstable bride vaulted onward to consuming *treyf,* unambiguously nonkosher food like ham, with a suspiciously oedipal zest.

Lobster, as rebarbatively *treyf* as a ham, was the emblem of their marriage. They honeymooned in Maine, tootling up the coast from lobster pound to lobster pound in a new roadster that was their wedding gift from Grandpa Joe Saltzman. Back in Detroit, one of their favorite restaurants became Joe Muer's, the giant seafood place on Gratiot, where lobster was always an option. But Daddy was in true lobster heaven when he took me and my sister to the Maine shore in the summer of 1959. We ate our way through one lobster pound after another, starting the meal with steamed clams and then ripping apart chicken lobsters at bare picnic tables outdoors, within a sniff of the Atlantic.

Daddy never tired of telling me how he loved this "animal" dining experience. That it might be not only a transgression against the civilized dining standards Mother maintained at home but also a thumb in the eye of kashruth did not seem to occur to him. He affected indifference to Judaism, but not toward his identity as a Jew.

On one of those rare occasions when he took me on an outing that didn't end up at a sports arena, we ate at a dingy deli called Lieberman's Blue Room. The light was actually bluish, from overhead fluorescent bulbs. And the dish I ordered also had a bluish tinge. The budding food critic foreshadowed his later forays into exotic comestibles by ordering *lungen,* a dispiriting bowl of spongy, stewed lungs.

I couldn't eat them. I don't think I could do it easily today, but there is no risk of a test, since lungs cannot be sold legally in the United States: abattoirs no longer inspect them for human consumption.

Lieberman's, despite its dismal decor, was a vibrant part of the old Dexter-Davison Jewish neighborhood, with its Ashkenazic immigrant flavor. When that increasingly affluent community fled an encroaching black population and resettled a few miles to the northwest, the Yiddishkeit of Dexter-Davison did not survive the move. The delis that did make it to Livernois and Seven Mile Road were sleeker and kosher in "style" only. Darby's and Boesky's (the family that produced the Wall Street felon Ivan, who mysteriously changed the pronunciation of his surname from the Bo-es-kee we all grew up with as customers to Bow-skee; he went to jail and the Boesky restaurants are gone) laundered the sometimes funky menu of places like Lieberman's. No more *lungen,* or *eiter* (udder) either.

Our family ate most of its out-of-the-home meals at a group of forgettable genteel places with refined and distorted versions of ethnic food, none of it decisively phonier than what you would have found back then in most second-rank American cities, but phonier and with a shakier claim on local tradition than famous places in New York, Chicago, San Francisco or New Orleans at the time.

When I was fifteen, I was happy to be fed overcooked pasta at Mario's, or greasy French-fried frog's legs at Fox & Hounds, the pseudo-British roadhouse in goyish suburban Bloomfield Hills. Years later these forays provided me with a baseline of well-meant culinary fraud against which to see how the real thing in France or Italy stood out as sharply different from the culinary dishes we ate on those Sunday nights out in the Motor City of the '50s.

Detroit was a backwater, but it did have two unique places to eat, one raffishly elegant and nationally acclaimed. The other was an eccentric burger joint disguised as a railroad train. I never ate at either one of them until I was in high school, and never with my family.

At the high end was the London Chop House, an eclectic downtown watering hole run by Les and Cleo Gruber, pals of James Beard's (he named their glittery '21' Club clone one of the ten best restaurants in the nation in 1961) and authors of an excellent guide to the restaurants of the world. The Chop House attracted Detroit's big shots, car guys and real estate honchos, exactly the crowd my glitz-shy parents shunned. They would, however, consent to eat across the street at the Grubers' less brash Caucus Club. Neither of the Gruber kitchens were temples of gastronomy. They didn't offer much more than top raw materials—beef, lobsters, lake fish—plainly prepared and sold for top dollar. You'd get your name monogrammed on the matches at the table, but the food chef Pancho Vélez cooked for both places was full of shortcuts and off-the-shelf flavorants. According to the food-history blogger Jan Whitaker, Pancho did not hesitate to jazz up carrots with maple-flavored syrup or to stir onion powder into mashed potatoes.

At the other end of the culinary scale, a retired adman named Bill Brooks served unremarkable hamburgers on a dreary stretch of Woodward Avenue somewhere between the city limits and Birmingham to the north. But Brooks was a true snob, unlike Les Gruber, who would serve anybody who'd pay his freight. You couldn't eat at Bill's unless he approved of you.

First of all, you had to be plugged in enough to know that the locomotive-shaped building with no sign on it was a restaurant. Then you had to understand that the chef-owner, a gray-haired recessive, had a microphone concealed near the locked, bell-less front door. Initiates would stand there calling out their names and pleading to be admitted. If he agreed and felt like working that night, Bill would buzz you in to a dark and ill-kempt vestibule that led to a small semicircular counter. The proprietor would emerge from his little hidden kitchen, make a stab at a congenial greeting and take your order.

Before long, an electric train rolled out of an opening in the kitchen wall on the track that ran along the counter. Your burgers sat on little flat cars. Bill stopped the train several times so that the flat car with the appropriate burger came to rest right in front of the person who'd ordered it.

I knew that this food, and the rest of what we were getting in local restaurants, was mediocre stuff. I had, after all, been to Chicago many times—twice with my family and on several other occasions while changing trains on my way to Camp Kawaga, near Minocqua, Wisconsin. So I knew what you got in a really big city at legendary addresses (Barney's, the stockyard steak house, and the slightly more sophisticated Fritzel's, a showbiz magnet in the Loop famous for "continental" dishes like chicken Vesuvio and steak Diane), and at the nationally known Polynesian "gourmet" chain Don the Beachcomber. We even passed through New York City once on our way back from that Maine idyll. But my first glimpses of high-end food, more or less authentically prepared, were at home.

Mother was an excellent and ambitious cook. Her repertoire was built on the German Jewish kitchen of her prosperous childhood in Detroit. Anyone who has looked at *The Settlement Cook Book* knows what we ate. The author, Lizzie Black Kander (1858–1940), gave cooking classes in a settlement house in Milwaukee to young immigrant Jewish women from eastern Europe. Her goal was to help these greenhorns cope with America. So in her lessons she combined German and Jewish specialties such as Bundt cakes and matzoh balls with more "American" recipes like blueberry gingerbread and salmon loaf. There was also a section called "Household Rules," a compendium of useful tips, such as how to maintain an icebox (a real one, with blocks of real ice; we had one like that ourselves at some point during World War II, stocked by an actual iceman, who cameth with large scary tongs).

Over the years and through many editions, Mrs. Kander actually increased the Jewish content of the book, perhaps sensing that much of her audience was, like my mother, already significantly assimilated and in need of grounding in the Jewish culinary heritage. Mother's own repertory far exceeded the limitations set by Mrs. Kander. She would boast that she could cook dinner for a month without ever repeating a dish.

Since we were entirely unobservant at home, dietary rules played no part in what we ate. My father was the only one of us with any trace of the shtetl, and he was an unhesitating adventurer at table. So my mother had a free hand to broaden her horizons as a cook, a project she conducted with help from *Gourmet* magazine.

I never ventured into her kitchen, except after dinner to dry

dishes on the maid's night out. It was Mother who boiled the artichokes and deep-fried the eggplant slices, trimmed the sweet-
breads and whisked together the hollandaise for the asparagus.

Wine did not appear in our house until I was in high school, a
bottle of pinkish Almaden, which loitered half-drunk in the refrigerator for many days. You may take this as a vestige of Jewish tradition if you like. I was in college when my father told me he had
just seen his first alcoholic Jewish patient.

Mother kept active in the kitchen well into her eighties, always
picking up new recipes. (The spicy pecans of her invention coincided with the craze for Asian fusion in the 1980s world-at-large.)

When I left home for two years of boarding at Cranbrook
School in Bloomfield Hills, a half-hour drive north of our last
house inside the city of Detroit proper, I had been exposed, without realizing it, to a fairly broad spectrum of foods and food ideas,
and I was inclined by my home training to opt for novel things to
eat when they were on offer. Cranbrook, an architecturally magnificent complex built for a Detroit newspaper millionaire by the
Finnish genius Eliel Saarinen, taught me many things—Latin
poetry, English hymns, French-kissing—but it was an interruption of my alimentary education.

School food is school food is school food. I do, however,
remember with affection a dessert we called anti-gravity pudding,
because you could invert the dish and its contents would not fall
onto the table. Cranbrook also taught me how to clear the entire
service for a table of twelve on a single tray without dropping a
glass or a saucer on the endless walk to the kitchen, past twenty-
four tables of malicious teenage boys hoping you would lose control of your cargo. The trick was to load the tray on a sideboard
so that most of the weight was piled on one side. Then you knelt
beside it, slid the heavy side over your shoulder and stood up,

very carefully. With practice, the tray could then be held with one hand, on the underweighted outer side, while the free hand swung smugly at one's waist.

It is also true that I learned to appreciate rum before graduation, but I don't count that as the beginning of real connoisseurship in the beverage department. Especially since my coindulger and I consumed the stuff with Coke and then got sick in a YMCA room far from school.

I didn't learn much about food at Harvard, either. My college diet consisted of more school food punctuated with cheap eats at restaurants in Cambridge and Boston. To be fair, you could, and I did, try whale steak at Chez Dreyfus. Chez Jean on Shepard Street introduced me to rillettes and other traditional French bistro food. There was gussied-up New England fare at Locke-Ober. But like a whole generation of future American food lovers, I discovered the gastronomic me on $5 a day (and often less) bumming around Europe after freshman year, in the summer of 1960.

Armed with $1,000 from savings and gifts, I joined an unofficial student invasion of the Old World, which had still not entirely rebounded from two world wars and an intervening economic collapse. This meant that dollar-holding ephebes like me could afford to eat every night in charming Left Bank bistros like Julien et Petit or La Chaumière. And if you were actually me, an inchoate food obsessive smothered by thirteen years of anti-gastronomic formal schooling, you devoured not only the *artichaut à la barigoule* (including the *fonds,* which you saw French diners at nearby tables extracting from the leaves and broth) but the concept of an orderly food heritage—a cuisine. After a summer of assiduously feeding off menus written in a language as traditional as the Homeric Greek I'd just learned to read at Harvard, I had signed on, without consciously knowing it, to a lifetime of passionate interest in filling my mouth and brain with as much of this previously undreamed of culinary material as my late start and physical distance from the source would allow.

The strong dollar also bought cheap travel, first by air and then by rail, to every other corner of Europe my meager cognitive map of the continent suggested as a destination. The Eurail Pass was my carte blanche to Spain, Germany, Holland, Belgium, Italy and even Greece. In only thirteen weeks, I chugged through a kaleidoscope of European capitals and second cities, spending the days in museums and the evenings at restaurants that functioned as survey courses in European cooking.

On an early August evening, I boarded not the Orient Express but a by-blow named the Simplon-Orient Express, because it passed through the Simplon Tunnel from Switzerland to Italy and then continued on through Yugoslavia to Athens. After four dismal, sooty, hungry nights on the train, I was back in my element, imbibing the food of Greece—the plethora of mezes, the lamb in all forms and, outstandingly, the supernal melons in the garden at the Byzantine monastery of Hosios Loukas in Boeotia.

Later that summer came the raspberries in Venice and Florence and Rome, *lamponi*, served with cultured, vaguely sour, thick cream or with sugar, but never both, unless you asked nicely.

So by the end of that thirteen-week sojourn in Europe, I had seen the *Mona Lisa* and the caryatids at the Erechtheum, St. Paul's Cathedral and the Rembrandts in Amsterdam. But what had been planned as a cultural "grand tour" on a student budget had turned into a voyage of gastronomic discovery, a self-taught survey course on the cuisines of Europe, with cultural landmarks crammed in between meals.

The most important research project came almost at the end of the "course." I went to Maxim's in Paris. It had three stars in Michelin, but an eighteen-year-old American with $20 could eat

there as if he were King Farouk. I ordered *caneton aux pêches,*
duckling with peaches, *not oranges.* The menu said the dish came
right out of Escoffier. Now, I thought, I was in touch with the
highest and best a person could experience, a variation on a great
French dish by the greatest of chefs; classic. And like those other
classic monuments of European culture, from Aeschylus to the
mansarded roofs of the Louvre, this culinary monument, and all
the hundreds of classic dishes I'd met with, were part of a tradition
that had gelled for the ages.

And you could eat it. Again and again.

With cuisine, as with classical literature, you had a fixed text,
or at least an archetypal recipe to which all those dishes I was eating arguably pointed back, just as the surviving manuscripts of
Catullus and Plato, altered by scribal recopying over the centuries, had a common ancestor. From this premise arose the concept of culinary authenticity, of getting things right in the kitchen,
reproducing the foods of France or Italy just as innocents abroad
like me and thousands of other young American travelers experienced them on their home grounds, guided by experts like Julia
Child or Marcella Hazan, meticulously faithful to tradition. But
as a firmer sense of the history of cuisines came over me, I slowly
came to see that the food I'd eaten in contemporary Europe had
evolved throughout the modern period. Certainly the food of
Europe before Columbus, tomatoless and potatoless, was nothing like the European food universe we knew, with its *salades de
tomates, potages Parmentier,* and on and on and on. You couldn't
even push back the dawn of authenticity as far as 1850, once you
began looking at cookbooks and other documentation of food
eaten in the nineteenth century and comparing it with the food of
our day. This turned out to be true even for societies assumed to
be glacially traditional, such as China and India.

But in the summer of 1960, it was bliss to believe that the cuisines I had been informally studying on a shoestring in restaurants all over western Europe were as immutable as the conjugation of Latin verbs.

I walked back from Maxim's to my Left Bank fleabag, stopping at a café for a game of pinball (*le flipper*). By then I knew the drill. First you asked the cashier for change—*de la monnaie,* if from a five-franc note; more often, you exchanged a franc coin for five twenty-centime pieces, *cinq pièces de vingt,* worth about four U.S. cents each, enough for five games (*parties*). Then you wormed your way next to the crowd of spectators around the Gottlieb pinball machine and plunked a coin down on the glass, asserting your right to play next.

One night I surpassed myself, flipping and nudging my way to a celestial score worth three free games. A tall North African had been watching me.

"*Pas mauvais, monsieur,*" he said. It was late. I had an early train to England and my flight home. I waved off the compliment and walked out, leaving the man to play my *parties gratuites.*

Two years passed. I studied more Greek and Latin. I spent another summer in Europe, three months filled with more classic meals, of which the highlight was a lunch with my parents and sister at France's most important and historically pivotal restaurant, La Pyramide, in Vienne, on the Rhône south of Lyon. The food world knew this elegant, three-star establishment as Chez Point, or simply Point. Its founder, Fernand Point, had died in 1955, but his wife, Mado, kept the place going without any decline that a naive twenty-year-old could perceive.

I was also unaware, as I suspect were most of the guests filling the sunny *terrasse* of Point in late July 1962, that Chef Point's legacy of light sauces and uncluttered plates would live on in the kitchens of his former apprentices, Paul Bocuse, the Troisgros brothers and virtually every other future star of the nouvelle cui-

Fernand Point, 1947: He purified the language of the French kitchen and passed on his leaner cuisine to the young chefs who then created nouvelle cuisine.

sine. What struck me was the *foie gras en brioche*. I had eaten *pâté de foie gras* before, usually an inert pink spread scooped out of a can. But inside this flawless brioche, the Point kitchen had inserted fresh unadulterated foie gras. On the plate was a deceptively unimposing round slice of liver surrounded by a golden ring of bread. The taste caught me by surprise. This, I saw, was the real thing, the rich and refined goose liver that all the fuss was about.

I can't recall the rest of the meal, only the very end, when my father discovered that his wallet was missing. He thought he must have left it in the car. I was sent out on a search mission. There it was on the driver's seat, unmolested.

Pierre (standing) and Jean Troisgros. In the pokey cattle town of Roanne, these former Point acolytes served the most radical and witty menu of the postwar period.

If I hadn't been so anxious about the wallet, I might have looked up the street and seen the Gallo-Roman pyramid (really an obelisk) that gave the restaurant its name.

By legend, Point had once tried to resolve an argument between two customers right there where our car was parked. He'd persuaded two men who were fighting over the lunch bill to take their loud dispute outside and decide the matter by racing on foot to the pyramid. The winning runner would pay the bill.

Point was the starter. Off the men ran. And ran and ran and ran, until they disappeared into the afternoon.

Back in Cambridge, I found senior year an abrupt culinary letdown but a big step up in the interpersonal relations department. By Labor Day I was married, and with the marriage came a kitchen. Mostly, my wife did the cooking, without any expectation that I would help out except with the dishes. But I did get my hand in, crucially, in the summer of 1964, in the easy weeks between my Fulbright year of reading classical greats at Wadham College, Oxford, and the onset of classics graduate school back at Harvard.

Our apartment was in student housing, across Kirkland Street from the home of Julia Child. I saw the already legendary Julia from time to time in the neighborhood. We even shared a butcher, Jack Savenor, a genial sort eventually accused of overstating the weight of his meat.

Julia and I didn't meet then, but I had her book, *Mastering the Art of French Cooking,* volume one. And I had the time to try its most challenging recipe, cassoulet, the Provençal bean stew with its numerous meats. In following through with more determination than finesse every one of its densely hortatory six pages, Margaret and I joined an avant-garde of ambitious home cooks whisking their way to authenticity with Julia as their chef.

Oh, yes, that cassoulet was a delicious success, and its combination of deliciousness and technical perfection, made possible by a recipe with consummate completeness and authoritative manner, reinforced my belief that great food was food prepared in the most traditionally accurate manner, with no crass substitutions like dried mushroom soup as a sauce base or inert mayonnaise spooned out of a bottle, and, on a higher plane, no deviations from tradition.

Long before the political scientist Francis Fukuyama declared that history had come to an end, every serious disciple of Julia's

Julia Child and her Cambridge butcher, Jack Savenor, 1966. I bought meat there when I was a Harvard graduate student in 1965, but I was too shy to introduce myself to my favorite cookbook author.

already had concluded (actually, without any specific instruction on this point from Mrs. Child) that the history of food had ground to a halt at some point before World War II. Culinary classics were a heritage we could study, but neither we nor the great chefs of Europe, who had learned the classic repertoire during long authoritarian apprenticeships, were going to tamper with the treasures in this edible museum.

There was, for example, only one basic way to assemble a roast of veal Prince Orloff. Julia's recipe starts with a reference to the master recipe earlier in the book for casserole-roasted veal. For veal Orloff the finished roast is sliced and then reassembled after being coated with a mixture of two sauces: soubise (pureed onions and rice) and duxelles (minced mushrooms). The reassembled roast is then coated with a third sauce: Mornay, which is a béchamel, or white sauce, thickened with cream and then flavored with grated Swiss cheese.

Julia spent a total of three detailed pages on this, but the professional chef's manual *Le repertoire de la cuisine* of Théodore Gringoire and Louis Saulnier (1914), a shorthand aide-mémoire based on Escoffier's *Le guide culinaire* (1903), which was still very much in use in later-twentieth-century French restaurant kitchens, dispatched the dish in four lines. But Gringoire and Saulnier prescribed intercalating the sauced slices with black truffle slices, and you were also sent scurrying to the specifications for *garniture Orloff,* a bevy of four intricate side dishes to be arrayed around the roast. Change any of this and you might as well have tried to pass off a cat as a dog.

What now sounds like stultifying fidelity to a tradition dating back not to the time of Vercingetorix, after all, but merely to the nineteenth century (to some point between 1856, when Czar Alexander II made Alexei Fedorovitch Orloff a prince in gratitude for his services as a diplomat in France, and Orloff's death, in 1862, when a celebrated French chef working in the princely kitchen in St. Petersburg invented veal Orloff) was universally accepted as the primordial state of French cuisine, immutable and for the ages. Perhaps no one ever said such a thing, but that is my point. Questions of historical change simply didn't come up. When they did, the notion of tradition and authenticity as granitic, almost prehistoric, unraveled and evolved into a more dynamic view of the origins of the cuisines we know.

I will confess that the prelapsarian, ahistorical point of view appealed to me. The idea that the world's greatest systems of cooking had not and would not be turned inside out by modernism, as literature and painting had been, attracted me just as strongly as the forever inviolable and unevolving literatures of antiquity had pulled me in.

Plato and *truite meunière* were both classics, in basically the same sense.

That is what I would have said if you had asked me about it back then. Anything worth calling a cuisine was as solid as a sedimentary rock built up over generations and centuries through the accretion of human experience in one culture over time. Of course, I wasn't stopping to think about all the constant change that had led to the supposedly granitic cuisines in existence circa 1970—the New World ingredients so seamlessly absorbed, the hundreds of dishes invented and published by nineteenth-century chefs like Antonin Carême. Perhaps because the previous sixty years in cooking had been stalled and kept from evolving by two world wars, an intervening depression and a slow recovery after the fall of Hitler, food history did seem to have ground to a halt. It was easy to believe that we had received a complete and unchanging constellation of recipes and foodways in the form of a cuisine, French or Italian and so on, that had its variations, as, say, ancient Greek had dialects, but the inherited aggregate, whether the Greek in dictionaries and in the surviving texts or French cooking in cookbooks or in surviving practice, was a finite system.

I fell into this way of thinking in Greek K, Harvard's class in advanced Greek composition, and I imbibed it at the feet of my undergraduate thesis advisor, the ascetic apostle of "slow reading," Reuben Arthur Brower.

Ben Brower had been my unofficial intellectual guru since freshman year. He was the senior faculty presence in Humanities 6, one of the general education courses you could choose from to satisfy a requirement Harvard created after World War II, to make sure that students didn't emerge from the increasingly specialized world of undergraduate instruction without a broad sense of civilization, especially Western civilization. Hum 6 tackled this job by teaching a method of literary criticism spun off from the rigorously ahistorical and objective method of reading sometimes called the New Criticism. Less dogmatic and radically skeptical than the French deconstructionism that did its best to kill the enjoyment of literature for a generation of student victims in the 1980s, Brower's version of New Criticism was really an invitation to pay close attention to the text you were reading. For a classicist—and Brower himself had started out as a classicist—Hum 6 wasn't all that different in approach from the philological analysis of Greek and Latin that scholars had been practicing since Hellenistic times.

For Brower, as for those early editors of Homer who clustered at the great library of Alexandria, a text was an enclosed, fixed object inviting purification and explication, not subjective reaction. Brower was himself not much given to subjectivity. The one overt expression of strong feeling I ever witnessed from him was therefore a real shocker. The week the television quiz show scandal broke around the Columbia English teacher Charles Van Doren in the fall of 1959, Brower walked into our small "section" class of Hum 6 (Harvard attempted to counter the formality of large lecture courses like Hum 6 with regular sections that permitted students to discuss the course material with a faculty member, usually a teaching assistant, but my great good luck had been to land in Ben Brower's own section) looking troubled. "What do you think of this Van Doren business?" he asked the class. There were various reactions, which eventually petered out. We were waiting to hear from Brower. He looked at the back of the little room, over our heads, and said, "If it were me, I would kill myself." Then he directed our attention to a passage from the book we were reading closely together, E. M. Forster's *Where Angels Fear to Tread.*

During senior year, I met with Brower nearly every week in the grand study-library that was his office in Adams House, the undergraduate residence where he was master. We talked of many things besides my thesis on *The Odyssey*, which he read with the same scrupulous attention he gave to all texts. It was a terrifying scrutiny—which, since he undoubtedly applied the same high standards to his own writing, explained in some measure why his scholarly output had been limited over the years, limited but diamond hard and exemplifying authority.

What I remember most clearly from those meetings was something Brower said about Greek composition, probably in reaction to my complaining about Greek K, which I found a dry exercise in turning English paragraphs into pastiches of Plato's Greek. Following the custom of centuries of students in this deliberately uncreative discipline, we were constrained to use only the exact vocabulary, grammatical constructions and syntax that Plato himself, the acknowledged master and model of classic Greek prose, had used.

Brower defended precisely what I deplored: "What would it mean to improvise an ancient Greek sentence? Greek is not an ongoing enterprise. It is only what the ancient Greeks wrote. The sole reason to compose sentences in Greek today is to revive, as best we can, their language, so that we can feel it as our own. That—in theory, at any rate—makes us better readers of Plato." There was no arguing with that. There was never any arguing with Reuben Arthur Brower, gentle man, with adamantine soul.

The lesson took. So when I thought about classic French food, another seemingly finite body of received culture, it was natural for me to think of it as I had been trained to think about dead languages. This was not a good analogy. As I soon realized, the most cursory look at early French cookbooks revealed a universe of cooking far removed from the haute cuisine system that grew up in the nineteenth century and that we had inherited in the form codified by Escoffier, a system that would shortly dissolve into a kaleidoscope of new, shimmering ideas before our dazzled eyes.

Even regional "cuisines" turned out to have histories. The "classic" dish of the Auvergne, in central France, the puree of potatoes and cheese called *aligot,* could not have been older than the introduction of potatoes into France from the Andes after Columbus. According to one theory, it was "originally" made with bread instead of potatoes, by monks who gave it to pilgrims on their way to Santiago de Compostela. Similarly, in Spain, gazpacho in its present tomato-based form could not have been cooked before the sixteenth century and probably emerged much later. Cervantes's gazpacho is not ours.

Pizza has a history, too. Of course, everything has a history. But that is not what was in my mind in the 1960s when I was discovering the food of Europe and the rest of the world. The historical attitude would come later. And I was also not describing the reality of my experience as an eater in those years when I maintained that my ecstatic gorging was some sort of cold-blooded investigation of a vast archaeological museum of human food culture.

In fact, I was just eating whatever piqued my interest, in restaurant after restaurant, country after country, region after region—and trying to taste as many dishes as I possibly could. I'm sure I never gave a thought, in the summer of 1960, my first time in Europe, to cuisines as calcified legacies. I was, of course, eating my way through the cuisines of Europe, but unsystematically, happily devouring the menu at hand.

My approach, instinctive, rabid and utterly natural, had much in common with language learning. As a matter of fact, I was operating in the same indiscriminate, sopping-up mode with French that summer, taking in every new word that came along, looking each one up obsessively in the dictionary, forcing myself to check every word I didn't know in the paperback of Dumas's *La dame aux camélias* I'd bought from a *bouquiniste* on the Quai Voltaire near my *hôtel garni*, thus acquiring a large vocabulary for discussing tuberculosis and coughing.

In restaurants, I acquired a huge new vocabulary of dishes, *andouillette, marcassin, cou d'oie farci aux lentilles, râble de lièvre*— none of which I had eaten before, or even known about in English; nor would I see them in America for decades. These dishes were a bit like the words for tubercular conditions in Dumas: not likely to be useful in my daily life in the States but part, nevertheless, of a growing collection of factoids that entered my consciousness, my self.

Obviously, my food experiences contributed more than lexical entries to my memory of those meals. I tasted every one of those dishes with gusto and could still give you a vivid account of the flavors and textures in many of them. But those sensations—the ugly technical term for them is organoleptic—were not the important ones. For me, they never have been of primary importance, except at the time I was experiencing them. What mattered most was the dish, in all its aspects.

Take *sole meunière.* Yes, I love this flat white fish's tender, smooth flesh and the way its mildness is set off by the lightly browned butter and the acid of the lemon juice it's cooked in. Because I have eaten the dish many times, I'm able, as a critic, to judge a restaurant's specific presentation, comparing it against others from my past. But even that kind of judgment rests primarily on my sense of what defines the dish, of what might be called its Platonic form in my mind.

I am thinking of a canonical sequence: four boned fillets

dredged in seasoned flour, quickly sautéed tableside in browned butter, which, just as the fish is cooked through, sizzles from the addition of the lemon juice. It is this sizzle, at the climax of the waiter's enactment of the dish, that defines my sense of *sole meunière*. I am also interested in the epithet *meunière*, collapsed from *à la meunière*, in the manner of a miller's wife. Like many French names for dishes, it is probably entirely fanciful. But the philologist in me can't help wondering if there once was some kind of connection, in folklore or in a chef's experience, that honored a miller's wife's way with a saltwater fish that was clearly not pulled up from the family millrace. Perhaps it was the flour coating, the miller's product.

Other people no doubt give their organoleptic memories pride of place. Not me. I am, first and last, attracted by the concept of the dish, its definition, the kinds of information you'd find in Gringoire and Saulnier's *Répertoire de la cuisine* or, for a more detailed description, in a standard recipe.

I have a philologist's sensibility. I see an unfamiliar term on a menu and I want to order that dish, add it to my vocabulary. In 2009, at the excellent Chicago restaurant Spiaggia, I spied the unfamiliar word *pagliolaia* on the menu. The waiter said it meant "dewlap." I thought of the hounds in *A Midsummer Night's Dream*: "Their heads are hung / With ears that sweep away the morning dew; / Crook-knee'd, and dew-lapp'd like Thessalian bulls; / Slow in pursuit, but match'd in mouth like bells."

Spiaggia cooked its dewlaps with diver scallops and wild mushrooms over a wood fire. I ordered the dish, amused that a midwestern chef was one-upping the trend for beef cheeks started by Mario Batali in New York with an even more arcane part of the bovine head. In my review, I hewed to the organoleptic: "The hearty beef fragments and earthy fungus highlight the slippery elegance of the seafood. Having dewlaps myself, I winced for a minute but sur-

rendered to the brilliance of the conception and the resourceful-
ness of Spiaggia's butcher." I did not disclose my white-magical
motivation for ordering *pagliolaia*, which was to learn a new word
by consuming the thing itself.

Did I realize back in 1960 or in the next two decades that I
was approaching food in this way? Undoubtedly not. I thought I
was ingesting cuisines, cultural artifacts frozen like the smiles on
archaic Greek statues. And when the smile melted, when those
gelid monoliths changed shape before my eyes, I continued to
see the change as a systematic mutation, a wholesale revolution,
which it was. But the revolution expressed itself through individual dishes, one recipe at a time. And that, of course, was how I
experienced the nouvelle cuisine and every one of the later con-
volutions that have transformed the way we eat, and continue to
transform it.

After I passed my PhD orals at Harvard, in the spring of 1965,
I got a chance to explore French food in great depth. Instead of
supporting myself as a teaching fellow in Cambridge while writing
my dissertation, I accepted a job as a correspondent in *Newsweek*'s
Paris bureau. In the early mornings before the office opened, I
researched the scholarly literature on Theocritus at the Biblio-
thèque Nationale. Later in the day, I researched the menus of
French restaurants.

Newsweek had hired me because someone at the magazine
believed it would locate abler staffers at America's better college
newspapers than it was finding among older journalists at professional papers and magazines. This turned out to be a false theory,
in the sense that almost every one of the *Harvard Crimson*–hatched
trainees except me left *Newsweek* for law school or other greener
pastures after a short stint at the magazine.

Fully expecting that I would return to academia, too, with a
completed thesis, I went to work in the *Newsweek* offices off the

Champs-Élysées. I ought to have been very busy, chasing news while simultaneously plowing through the scholarly literature on Hellenistic poetry of the third century B.C. In fact, I had almost no news to chase, and the Theocritus scholarship was almost completely irrelevant to my specific interest in the father of pastoral poetry's creative reuse of rare Homeric words. Previous researchers had not spent much time on this question, which allowed me to flip through and discard hundreds of articles brought to me by disgruntled stack "boys" of advanced age every weekday morning. Soon there were no more tomes to check out. I had stumbled onto untilled ground, but by then I had lost interest in academic life and tabled the thesis.

In the bureau, I was the fourth of four correspondents, and the youngest by far at twenty-four. In the French idiom, I was the office *benjamin* (after Joseph's youngest brother in the Old Testament). In practice, this meant that, aside from reading seven daily newspapers and thirty magazines, I had almost nothing to do. The other three correspondents, better connected, more skilled and more aggressive, hogged all the available work. And there wasn't much of that, considering the very small amount of its precious space that *Newsweek* would allot to a backwater like France in a normal week.

Even French reporters didn't have much of a story to follow then, because France under President Charles de Gaulle was essentially a benevolent dictatorship. De Gaulle had a chokehold on the news. In this quasi-totalitarian atmosphere, a very junior American correspondent had almost no chance of breaking stories major enough to interest a stateside editor. I had to plead to get the bureau to submit my name for accreditation to the only major event of my two years in France, a De Gaulle press conference, which one of the veteran correspondents would actually cover.

Yet I was a full-fledged foreign correspondent with a very

official-looking clothbound press card and, fatefully, an expense account. So I busied myself with entertaining "sources" (most often just friends with marginally newsworthy job descriptions) at restaurants of high gastronomic quality. No one in the office minded. In fact, the bureau chief seemed glad not to have me nagging him for work, and it amused my colleagues that I was putting so much energy into establishing contacts in corners of French life they had no time to investigate.

When I left for a job in the New York headquarters, in 1967, the bureau gave me a copy of the antiquated but still respected *Larousse gastronomique* as a token of my colleagues' respect; or perhaps it was their mildly scornful recognition of my being a person for whom food was a passion.

I had eaten at the big-name restaurants, the three-stars, which were venerable exercises in period performance. Chez Maxim was all deco froth. Lapérouse specialized in Gilded Age naughtiness, with dining alcoves that could be closed off from public view by pulling a drape to hide you and your *poule de luxe*. The Tour d'Argent gave you a card inscribed with the number of the *canard à la presse* they had just served you. Mine, I believe, was the 22,987th to be crushed and exsanguinated in that calf-sized silver device that glittered at one edge of the dining room high above the Seine with its famous view of Notre-Dame. On the street level was an actual museum, featuring menus from the Paris Commune of 1871, when the Tour d'Argent had served its besieged patrons with the flesh of animals "liberated" from the zoo of the Jardins des Plantes, a few blocks away.

The closest a *fin bec* could get to a creative sensibility in a high-end Paris restaurant in 1967 was either at glamorous Lasserre, near our office, or at Chez Garin, the remarkable bistro near my Left Bank apartment. Lasserre had a mechanical roof that opened to the sky in warm weather, to provide relief from the heat and to clear the accumulated Gauloise smoke from the elegant room. Tables sported costly articulated metal birds, which the intoxicated sometimes tried to purloin, under the waiters' watchful eyes. It was part of the fun to see some pinstriper caught red-handed with a glittery peacock or snipe in his briefcase. The food was first-class and vibrantly *cuisiné*, showing the hand of a chef not yet ready for the mortuary.

Garin wasn't so flashy, but for a lot of money you got top-flight versions of conventional cooking tuned up and rethought, sometimes with enough complication so that they really edged across the line into haute cuisine, or made the boundary between bistro and haute cuisine seem beside the point. Gael Greene ate there in May 1972 for *New York* magazine, about the last moment when any major French restaurant could still elicit ooh-la-las for trout stuffed with a pike mousse. The influence of the nouvelle cuisine's great young chef Michel Guérard was already visible, if unavowed, in the two vegetable purees (celeriac and string bean) that Garin served Ms. Greene as a garnish for a split grilled kidney.

Just five years earlier, the nouvelle cuisine revolution had already begun simmering in the provinces. My bureau chief, Joel Blocker, proposed a story about someone named Paul Bocuse who was making news just outside Lyon. Joel struck out with his Bocuse proposal, but he would have been able to win space in the magazine for another modern French chef also trained by Fernand Point, if sudden political news hadn't sidetracked him and forced him to send me instead to a small town in Alsace for the announcement of a third Michelin star to L'Auberge de l'Ill in tiny Illhaeusern.

Although the article on the restaurant that appeared in *Newsweek*'s April 3, 1967, edition was unsigned, it was nonetheless my debut as a food writer. The food I ate on this fateful assignment included a spit-roasted *poularde de Bresse* with truffles and golden

Restaurant Paul Bocuse at Collonges-au-Mont-d'Or, which features culinary innovation in a flamboyant atmosphere.

Alsatian noodles. I have no memory of how it tasted or what it looked like, but it was clearly an attempt by the chef, Paul Haeberlin, to combine the very best chicken he could find with a luxury ingredient necessary to legitimize the dish as worthy of three stars, a cooking method that set it apart from everyday oven-roasted chicken. The noodles, a regional specialty, added handmade, local distinction. This, in itself, was a daring modernism, a belated nod to the automobile age. Haeberlin had bet his future that garnishing his signature chicken with humble noodles instead of an array of elaborately turned vegetables out of the *Larousse gastronomique* would appeal to Michelin's modernizing inspectors.

This discreet nod to the Auberge's remoteness from Paris, in a village so small it had no hotel, in a province whose identity was not securely French, would have resonated immediately with the Michelin inspectors looking for a rationale to justify adding this modest-looking hostelry to the pantheon of twelve three-star temples it had been enshrining almost without change for years. But, as neither they nor I could have said at the time, this dish, semiotically complex as it was (high/low, rustic/elegant, cosmopolitan/regional, French/German), would not count, when examined by hindsight anytime after 1972, as a forerunner of the radical changes soon to disrupt French kitchens. History was accelerating for chefs.

For me, the Illhaeusern reportage was important and memorable because of two other historically trivial reasons. It gave me a taste of food journalism, and it gave my son Michael, then on the verge of two, a taste of a really good soft-boiled egg.

I was traveling with him and my wife, Margaret, because the assignment had burst upon me on the eve of a skiing vacation. We piled into a rental Peugeot station wagon and drove due east through Nancy to Alsace. I had left Margaret and Michael in the hotel at nearby Ribeauvillé, thinking it would be unprofessional to bring them along for an interview at the restaurant. But when Jean-Pierre Haeberlin, Paul's brother, who ran the front of the house, learned they were nearby, he insisted that Margaret and Michael be fetched for lunch.

Paul prepared a special meal for our infant, the egg and some remarkable mashed potatoes. When the egg appeared, Michael took a look at the amazingly reddish-orange yolk and exclaimed, "Apricot." A gourmet had announced himself. When he finished eating, two school-age daughters of Jean-Pierre's came out in regional costumes and led our boy upstairs for a nap.

Could this kind of unaffected hospitality survive the onslaught of adult gourmets in diamonds and limos? Jean-Pierre Haeberlin was justifiably worried. He said (and *Newsweek* quoted him):

> We want to keep our simple country spirit, but from now on everything will have to be more expensive. We'll need more help, a wider cheese selection, nothing but the choicest fruit. The higher prices will keep away some of our local clientele. To make up for that, we'll have to draw many more tourists and that means we'll be dealing with a more modish crowd. Between you and me, I don't think we're ready for the third star yet.

It was also a moment of challenge and change for me. Despite this minor triumph in Alsace, and a more significant professional success with an interview I extracted from Orson Welles when his Shakespearean film *Chimes at Midnight* opened in America, my career as a Paris correspondent had not flourished. I brooded over that with the typical paranoia of someone working at the periphery of a large organization. Was I being stifled by a hostile bureau chief who felt I had been foisted on him by his bosses in New York? I thought so. And when Jack Kroll, the senior editor in charge of cultural coverage, invited me to return to New York and work for him in the "back of the book," where I had flourished as a trainee two years earlier, I did not hesitate to accept his offer.

Margaret was too far along in her second pregnancy to fly, so she and I and little Michael booked passage on the *France*. The meals were grand. I remember one breakfast with retrospective astonishment: course after course, including an omelet with asparagus tips peeking coyly out from one end and kidneys roasted in their own fat. Mostly, we slept between meals. A Frenchman we met on board attributed this doziness to the gentle undulation of the ship. *"Le tangage,"* he said. *"Ça endort."* (The ship's pitching puts you to sleep.)

I blamed the duck at lunch.

After five halcyon days on a sunny, placid North Atlantic, we landed at the docks on the West Side of Manhattan on my twenty-sixth birthday, August 1, 1967, unsure if I'd made the right decision.

I knew that if I had stayed on much longer in France, I would likely have made my life there. My spoken French was taking over my English as the language in which I found it easier to express myself. So much of my brief adult life had occurred in French. There were already subjects I had first learned about in the language. We had made friends. Michael was becoming a French child.

When I'd made the decision to leave Paris, it had seemed clear that if we did not return home then, we would likely find ourselves increasingly confirmed as expatriates. This vision had a certain appeal for me. I had worked hard to adjust to Paris and was proud when the very senior French reporter Michel Gordey told me that summer that I had made a good *"début."* But it wasn't enough. For a grandchild of refugees, "expatriate" was just a fancy word for "immigrant." And however fluent and idiomatic my French became, it would always be a second language for me. There would always be words whose genders I'd be unsure about, cultural references I wouldn't get, anti-American remarks I'd feel obliged to object to even if I basically agreed with them. Worst of all, my child would be a native speaker—in fact, a native in all respects except his place of birth. And I would be the slightly awkward foreign parent, subtly out of place.

Yet we felt just as *dépaysé* in those first few weeks in New York. Homeless, with a birth just weeks away and a confusing and ill-defined new assignment at *Newsweek,* I was as anxious about my life as ever. The apartment we found was a charmless box in an ugly newish building. Its windows looked out on the building behind. Through them, we could see a couple our age conducting their lives just a few yards away.

One of our first nights in this place, my parents came to dinner. Midway through the soup, Mother gasped and pointed to the window. Our neighbors were demonstrating the missionary position. They kept it up through our main course, interrupting their revels from time to time to sweep the floor and comb their large mutt.

Dinner out in Manhattan was much less exhilarating. We had been right to suspect the worst of the restaurant scene there. The bistros, a sorry gaggle of tired, hackneyed little dumps clustered near the theater district, served depressing retreads of clichés such as *canard à l'orange* or *coq au vin*. After trying one or two, we headed for the top, La Caravelle, which turned out to be a stylish oasis for high-society diners. *Town & Country* magazine had recently published a map of the restaurant's seating plan, complete with the names of chic patrons at their favorite locations in the room. We expected to be seated in the inner clutch of undesirable tables known as Siberia. We did not expect to find the menu as uninspiring as it was. Worst of all, we did not feel as though we were in a French restaurant of the sort you'd find in France, even though the menu's first language was French, as was the language spoken by the waiters.

Among the hors d'oeuvres at Caravelle (as at most of the other high-end French restaurants in town) were those pike dumplings known as *quenelles de brochet*, elegant specialties of Lyon virtually ubiquitous in the New York culinary stratosphere. There was a simple explanation for the curious local passion for *quenelles*. Behind them, and the menus at almost all the top French restaurants, lay the remarkable success of one man, Henri Soulé. He had created the restaurant in the French pavilion at the 1939 World's Fair and then re-created it as a permanent restaurant in 1941, Le

Pavillon, having acquired special immigrant status for himself and his staff as war refugees. *Quenelles* were a Pavillon trademark.

They also became a trademark of the various spin-offs and clones of Le Pavillon that sprang up in the ensuing decades. Soulé's snobbery was a defining part of what passed for haute cuisine in New York. He whored after big money and big names and sent those he considered nobodies to his back room. The already alienated ordinary gastronome could not help but see a tinge of anti-Semitism in Soulé's most celebrated mistreatment of a customer, his vendetta against Harry Cohn, who was the landlord of Le Pavillon but couldn't get a good table there.

The sole exception to the Soulé spirit in fancy French restaurants in New York in 1967 was a classy but not frosty restaurant in the garden of an East Side town house called Lutèce. The chef, André Soltner, had been a rising star in Paris when the French-American perfume heir and bon viveur André Surmain hired him to come to America and open a great restaurant. Lutèce, in my opinion at the time, was the only authentic French kitchen of high quality in the city. It was also not fragrant with disdain for its customers. The reason for this, according to Soltner's main competitor, Roger Fessaguet, the chef at Caravelle, was that nobodies were the only clientele Lutèce could attract. Fessaguet told me in an interview in 1973 that there were only two serious French restaurants in New York, his and Lutèce: "We get high society and Soltner gets everybody else."

This was a major exaggeration by that date, but it was certainly the case as late as 1971, when I met a man, Jewish but apparently not too happy about it, who confided to me that it was hard to take André Surmain seriously because he had changed his name from Sussman. There was also the problem of André Soltner's accent. It wasn't "really" French. He was Alsatian and sounded vaguely German when speaking English.

André and Simone Soltner with staff, 1981. This was Lutèce at its zenith, the nation's best restaurant and the last fully French establishment to occupy that position.

The other food I did come to love in those days in New York was a special kind of Chinese food, the spicy cuisine of Sichuan Province. There were no Sichuan restaurants as such yet, but Sichuan dishes had begun appearing at the Four Seas, located not in Chinatown but on a dark corner at the edge of the financial district on Maiden Lane.

The Four Seas restaurant was the project of a Chinese-Brazilian shipping magnate named C. Y. Tung. He was a fan of Sichuan cuisine and saw to it that a handful of typical Sichuan dishes appeared on the otherwise northern Chinese menu of the Four Seas. I was taken there by friends from graduate school, the sinologist John Schrecker and his wife, Ellen, who had eaten the real thing in Taiwan and eventually brought back with them a cook born in Sichuan.

All of this—the tyranny of Soulé's snobbish mediocrity, Soltner's scorned superiority, the occult rise of Sichuan cooking—struck me as good material for an article, and I wangled an assignment at *New York* magazine. The piece got as far as galley proofs before it was spiked because of a revolt by the magazine's permanent food staff, which included Gael Greene, a bodacious Detroiter from my old neighborhood, and her "underground gourmet" colleagues, the graphic designers Milton Glaser and Jerome Snyder. *New York*'s legendary editor Clay Felker exhibited no shame in telling me this, and he then went on to question my expense account as excessive. I was indignant. Whether he relented on the expenses, I do not recall. But it was clear—I was told directly by a *New York* managing editor—that, because of my prickliness, Felker had blacklisted me.

I had already been published as a food writer in 1965, in *Newsweek*, with a review of a cookbook, in which I included an account of a meal I'd cooked from its recipes. *The Connoisseur's Cookbook,* by Robert Carrier, was a compendium of food served at the American expat's trendy London restaurant, Carrier's. The review was signed. It was my debut in the food field, and the only published credit as a food writer I could show, when my life took, as they say, a dramatic turn.

I'd spent most of my time during that period reviewing books for *Newsweek*. They tended to be serious books, novels by Philip

Roth, exposés of the State Department. I also wrote cover stories about important writers: Ross Macdonald, Norman Mailer. I had a nice life.

Then one morning in the spring of 1971, another *Newsweek* cultural writer, Alex Keneas, came into my office with an idea so preposterous that I didn't even bother to reject it. I immediately forgot what he'd said.

What he said was: "Craig Claiborne is retiring as food editor of the *New York Times*. You should apply for the job."

Alex knew this because he had once worked as an editor on the society-obituary desk at the *Times* and he was still in touch with old friends at the paper—and he was aware of my obsession with food. As far as I was concerned, however, I had no claim on the most important job in American food journalism. I was, in today's terms, a foodie, but not a food professional. Certainly, I couldn't have gotten the *Times* to listen to me on my own, even if I had wanted to be a food critic.

But Paul Zimmerman could. Paul was *Newsweek*'s film critic, and, in an earlier phase, he had once interviewed Charlotte Curtis. The two of them, neighbors in Greenwich Village, had ended up as friends. Alex told Paul about his suggestion to me. Paul, whose dining experiences in Europe the previous summer I had helped plan, believed I would be an excellent replacement for Claiborne. He called up the redoubtable Curtis, who was under serious pressure from Claiborne to find his replacement so that he could get on with launching an independent newsletter.

One morning in the winter of 1971, Zimmerman came into my office and said, "I've been talking to Charlotte Curtis about you and the *Times* food job. She'd like to take you to lunch. Here's her number."

I called it. Why not? (Fateful words.) Why wouldn't I want to be taken to lunch by the acerbic and powerful Miss Curtis?

We met at La Côte Basque, Henri Soulé's second Manhattan restaurant, a gift for his mistress, Henriette Spalter, known in the restaurant trade as Madame Pipi, because, I was told, she had started out as the ladies' room attendant at Le Pavillon.

True to form, for a Soulé restaurant, the best seats at La Côte Basque were those near the street door. Charlotte and I sat at the table closest to the entrance, practically in the coat-check room.

The subject of food never came up. But Leonard Lyons did. He was cruising the dining room, pad in hand, gleaning tidbits for his syndicated *New York Post* gossip column, "The Lyons Den." We dodged his questions. A few minutes later, a bottle of white wine arrived, the gift of a turbaned Romanian dowager at a table a few feet away, who wanted to know who the young man with Charlotte Curtis was. We dodged her question, too. Farther down the wall of banquettes, I espied two luminaries well known to me who I hoped wouldn't espy me. They were Kermit Lansner, the editor of *Newsweek,* and Katharine Graham, chair of the Washington Post Company, which owned *Newsweek.*

Charlotte dropped me back at *Newsweek* in a cab that couldn't have taken more than three minutes to cover the ten blocks downtown from La Côte Basque. It was time enough, however, for her to get to the point: "You could probably have this job if you want it," she said. "But since you've never written about food or restaurants, you'll have to do some tryout pieces. We'll pay you for them, of course, and cover your expenses. The whole thing will be completely confidential. Are you interested?"

"Why not?" I replied.

Where was the harm? Why wouldn't I want to eat out on the *Times* and get paid for my trouble, which amounted to writing three short pieces that couldn't be spiked because they weren't supposed to be printed? It all seemed like some surreal lark. I assumed the *Times* would never hire me.

I told my wife exactly that. And my colleague Charles Michener also told me exactly that. His Yale friend Bill Rice, who had professional food training and lots of food clips, was clearly a better candidate.

But we were both wrong.

A few weeks after the Côte Basque lunch, after I'd handed in two restaurant pieces and an interview with Piper Laurie, then the wife of *Newsweek*'s movie critic Joe Morgenstern, about her baking skills, Charlotte Curtis called me at home. I was in the Forty-second Street library checking citations for a book I'd translated from French to be called *Imperialism Now*. It was an updating of Lenin's 1917 tract *Imperialism: The Highest Stage of Capitalism* written by a French economist of Maoist tendencies called Pierre Jalée. His previous book had been *The Pillage of the Third World*.

I had spent hundreds of hours at this task for a pittance, acquiring a transient competence in French financial lingo, including the French equivalents for "mutual fund" (*fonds communs de placement*) and "carbon black" (*le carbon black*). My publisher was a Nigerian, and his firm was called Third Press. I'd met him at a party and agreed to translate the Jalée book so that I could tell my lefty friends from Harvard, who accused me of selling out to the capitalist press, that I worked for *Newsweek* to support my Maoist activities.

This is not what I told Curtis. When I called her back, she wanted to know why I was in the library. I made something up.

"Congratulations," she said.

Pause.

"You are going to take the job, aren't you?"

"Why not?"

Two

The Ungastronomical Me

In the month I insisted on taking off before starting work at the *Times*, I spent much of each day worrying about what lay ahead. I knew I was about to take a blind leap. My wife wouldn't let me forget that. She knew that I was radically, hopelessly unqualified for the job, because she was an excellent cook, and she knew me to be an enthusiastic novice, at best. If I really did go to the *Times*, the world would assume, or expect, that I was an expert, self-taught perhaps, but with years at the stove behind me. There'd be no way I could fake that, not for long. If people came to our house for dinner, did I expect Margaret to pretend I'd made the dinner she'd actually prepared?

I'm a journalist, I countered—an observer, not a participant. Does anyone care if Clive Barnes can dance? As the *Times* ballet critic, his pirouettes were verbal.

Yes, she snapped back, but he'd spent his life studying pirouettes and arabesques. He was an informed observer. I was hardly his equivalent in food.

In fact, my fears were largely unfounded. After an initial bit of hazing from a couple of TV reporters, I settled into the job and

"We can only hope he's not the Times' new food man."

The *New Yorker* salutes me with a cartoon that preserves my anonymity.

discovered that both *Times* readers and even food professionals were eager for a fresh voice. Also, I had a test cook to make sure that the recipes published under my name actually worked.

Forty years later, I've been able to look back on my first thirty years of life and pick out strands and seams that connect with the person who jumped out into the public food arena in 1973 and stayed there from then on. But the embryonic gastronome I've been able to unearth with hindsight is a character no one back then could have predicted would remain anything but an intellectual with a side interest in food.

At a retirement brunch for an editor at the *New York Times Book Review* just after my appointment as food editor had been announced, Pauline Kael, the *New Yorker*'s movie critic, looked up from her bagel as I came into the room. "Since when did you become a food queen?" she asked.

If you had told me then that I would spend the rest of my life writing and reporting on food in major publications and in many books, I would have laughed at you. The real me was the guy checking citations in the library for his translation of *Imperialism Now*. I was the serious professional reviewer of books for *Newsweek* and the *New York Times Book Review*. The even more fundamental me was the Harvard and Oxford classics scholar, the polyglot, polymath culture maven, a journalist and man of letters, literally, a spelling champ.

My first-grade teacher, a charmless martinet named Smart, was the first to notice my gift. I had figured out how to read on the first day of school. It just hit me that the letters, which I'd already memorized at home, were clusters of sounds that made up words. But I quickly saw further that this was not always perfectly the case. Some letters were "silent." Some combined in completely unphonetic groups, groups that themselves were not always pronounced in the same way. But unlike most beginning readers, I saw right away that the exceptions themselves usually formed patterns.

"Through" could not be sounded out if you relied purely on the basic sounds of its letters, but concluding that o-u-g-h always sounded like "oo" did not help you pronounce the words spelled t-o-u-g-h or b-o-u-g-h. One rule wasn't enough, but three rules pretty much showed you the way to cope in this maze of muddling signs.

I saw this in a flash. I figured out, in an extremely exciting couple of days when I was barely six, that the apparently irrational business of spelling was not the chaos it seemed to everyone else struggling with it in my class. They were looking for a system to explain the deep mystery of Dick and Jane. I understood intuitively that there were many "systems" at work on those idyllically illustrated pages.

The more pages I read, the more little orthographic patterns emerged. So I read a lot, not consciously to bone up on spelling. I read because I could, and, because it was easy for me, I loved it. Mrs. Smart noticed and told other teachers. I had become what they thought of as a natural speller. This weird talent would not have been remarked upon if other children hadn't needed classroom practice to improve their spelling. But I quickly emerged in those drills as some kind of prodigy.

Show me the word "antidisestablishmentarianism" and I could spell it right away, even though I had no notion of what it meant and couldn't possibly have understood a dictionary definition without an hour of explanation of the history of the relations between church and state in nineteenth-century England. I doubt I had any firm idea of any of the parts of that phrase: century, nineteenth century, England, state, church. I was only a six-year-old, but I could spell "antidisestablishmentarianism" and a lot of other sesquipedalian jawbreakers, for the amusement and wonder of teachers and older children.

One day, I got taken into an eighth-grade homeroom to give a demonstration of my powers. The teacher was large and raven-maned, notorious in our school for, shall we say, threatening exuberance. Her students were giant thirteen-year-olds who looked to me like somebody's parents. They called out words and I spelled them.

So at six I tasted fame, and liked it. Word of my skill got around. My classmates joined the rest of the school in regarding me as a little resident genius. Neither they nor I would learn the phrase "idiot savant" until years later. So from then on, in my little world at the Hampton School in affluent northwest Detroit, I was the smartest kid.

There was some truth to my reputation for intelligence. I had unconsciously analyzed the English language's multifarious orthography, without having any sense of how all those vestiges of Latin, French and German—languages with more orderly but dissimilar spelling systems—had left their mark on the way our words looked. So I was intelligent when judged by real criteria, but in first grade I was rewarded for being able to perform a stunt. That was just the beginning.

In fifth grade, ever more adept at spelling ever more difficult words, I moved up from being a local prodigy to the higher and far more confusing status of national celebrity.

Every spring, all students in the five counties of the Detroit area who were enrolled in grades five through eight competed in a spelling bee sponsored by the *Detroit News*. First there was a competition for each grade, then for the entire school, then for a group of schools in the same district. District winners competed for the Detroit title. And the Detroit winner went to Washington, D.C., for the National Spelling Bee.

I was ten. I won my grade. I won my school bee and the district bee, and then the city bee. As I moved up the ladder, I got progressively more attention in the *News*, which paid for the whole circus as a promotional effort to attract readers.

After I was city champion, I came to know the Boys and Girls page editor of the *News*, a lively, smart, single, behatted, old-fashioned newshen named Virginia Schnell. Her most important assignment every year was the spelling bee, a sweet sinecure involving a week in Washington on the *News*'s tab, but the downside was spinning out usable copy about that year's city champion speller again and again, which meant spending many days with the moppet and his parents. But with me, Schnell hit the jackpot: I was quotable and often got her on the front page of the *News*. It got me fatally interested in journalism.

In Washington, I did better still for her. In 1952, at ten, I was the youngest contestant in the history of the bee. So I was mentioned in all the stories written by dozens of reporters for papers from coast to coast, and they were careful to say that I was representing the *Detroit News*. That was the protocol, since the reporters all understood that the real point of the exercise was to sell newspapers. They therefore attached each speller's newspaper sponsor to his name like some Homeric epithet: Minnie Mintz (*Akron Beacon Journal*), Billy Batson (*New York World-Telegram and Sun*).

Not only was I the youngest, I was also up to the competition. I finished twenty-second, and would have gone further if the pronouncer (the man who spoke each word we had to spell) hadn't mispronounced the word I missed. He looked at "assonance," a word he confessed he didn't know, and then said "A-sonance." He was quickly corrected but I, never having seen the word either, thought he'd unwittingly given me a clue. If it had two *s*'s, then any fool would have pronounced its first syllable to rhyme with "lass." But the pronouncer's first impulse had been to give it a long *a*, something normally possible only if there were only a single *s* following the *a*. Or so I reasoned before I went down misspelling "assonance" a-s-o-n-a-n-c-e.

This was not the end of it. In 1953, I returned to Washington as the Detroit champion and finished second, once again a casualty of official mispronunciation. That year the word was "spermaceti," pronounced by the very same official pronouncer as if it were a pasta: "spermacetti," like "spaghetti." I cried briefly before taking cover in the basement of the Commerce Department building, where the bee took place, among aquariums filled with salamanders slumbering in green-tinged tanks. My tears got on national television. I appeared on the front page of the *New York Times*, a distinction I never achieved while working there.

Since I was much better copy than the fourteen-year-old from Arizona who came in first, the Bee's administrator offered to send my mother and me to New York to be on *The Ed Sullivan Show* with the winner. We said no thank you, reminding him that the New York junket was supposed to be a special treat for the winning speller.

I was also told the name of the proofreader's manual from which the bee selected the words that contestants had to spell. This was, for someone at my level as a kid speller, a dead giveaway. If I returned the following year, as the man who leaked the word list source to me hoped, all the other children would be spelling words they'd never heard or seen, words such as "vigesimal," which I had guessed correctly that week had an *s* like "infinitesimal," instead of a *c* like "decimal." But with that secret list in hand, I'd have no more need for guessing. I could easily memorize every possible word they'd use in the next bee. It wouldn't matter if the pronouncer mangled every one. Only a slip of the tongue by me could keep me from the title.

But that would have been wrong. We went back to Detroit without going on *The Ed Sullivan Show*, and I never entered another spelling bee. I had retired.

But my reputation lived on. There I was in 1954 with two other thirteen-year-olds on a Woodward Avenue bus, making a racket. A dour biddy got up and came over to me. "Everyone knows who you are," she said. "So behave. What one Jew does reflects on all other Jews."

I switched to private school and escaped the community that knew my saga best. So my life as a teenager was fairly normal, but my academic résumé was stellar, and I believed in it.

If you graduate first in your class in high school and continue on to get a summa in classics at Harvard (picking up the undergraduate thesis prize and a junior year Phi Beta Kappa key along the way), you can be pardoned for thinking your brain is in good working order and ought to be the tool you use to make your way in the world.

That was my working theory of me. But as I reached adulthood and had to decide more precisely what to do with that tool, I began to doubt that my future lay in the classroom teaching Greek and Latin. I looked around myself, at the other graduate students and, with panic, at my teachers. My strings did not vibrate sympathetically with theirs. I loved Greek literature, and I had given it my best, for seven years. Now I needed a way out, and *Newsweek* came to the rescue.

Thank God for those movie reviews in the *Harvard Crimson*, which legitimized me in the eyes of the *Newsweek* recruiter. Without them, I would now be a disappointed retired professor of Greek at some provincial university. Instead, I landed a job in big-time journalism, where destiny put me in the way of Alex Keneas, who deftly put me in the way of Charlotte Curtis, who mistook me as the answer to her urgent need to hire a food man.

Three

Food News

"What will you be doing here?" asked the nice young woman in personnel whom I went to see after my welcoming lunch with Craig Claiborne and Charlotte Curtis.

"I'll be handling food," I replied.

"Well, I'll put you down as an N2."

I shrugged. As an elite news staffer, I had been put on the so-called publisher's payroll, which brought with it special, if largely ceremonial, privileges at the bank down the block, and saved me the indignity of dealing with the weekly paychecks that were the lot of less illustrious news slaves. I was to be paid each month.

When I finally received my first paycheck, it was suspiciously tiny, much less than the salary I'd been offered. I inquired. The nice lady in personnel had taken me at my word. When she'd seen that I was young and I'd said I was to be handling food, she'd made me an N2, an assistant salad handler in the cafeteria. We sorted it out.

In fact, I had inherited a little empire several floors above the *Times* newsroom. The phrase "splendid isolation" might have been coined to describe the food department. While the newsroom was making history by printing the Pentagon Papers, a leaked official study of the Vietnam War and its failures, I luxuriated in my peaceable kingdom. The most splendid of all its appurtenances was the test kitchen, whose professional-style Garland range, immaculate expanse of butcher block counters and forest of heavy-gauge copper pots came with an English test cook and a Polish maid to clean up after her.

The test cook, Jean Hewitt, was handsome, a diplomate in home economics from London, and quietly furious that I'd gotten the job she thought, with some real justice, she deserved more than I did. My staff also included a secretary, Velma Cannon, a very refined black lady of late middle years devoted to the white southern gentleman who'd previously occupied my desk. Last, but crucial to our ability to respond to the flood of mail that rolled in every day, was the stenographer, Anita Rizzi.

When the phone rang in that office my first day, I reached for the receiver at my elbow, but Anita beat me to it. Part of her job was to be the first responder. And if she was already on the line, Velma picked up the next call. If Velma and Anita were both busy with calls and still another rang, Jean took that one. I was last in this inverted pecking order, answering the phone at my desk only if the other three were already handling our ever-inquisitive readers. No one ever explained this to me. But I soon figured it out and fell in line. And like the others, when I answered a call, I said, "Food news."

I thought it was funny. Downstairs, where the real reporters were, they covered the news. We "covered" fast-breaking recipes and the policy decisions of chefs.

My irony was misplaced. Even though a great deal of what the *Times* food editor wrote about was not newsworthy, a crucial part of it, as Claiborne had defined the job, really was food news. My respect for him grew as I read through his old articles in the office files. He had discarded the old food-page model of recipes handed out by food product companies and restaurant "reviews" redacted from press releases or based on meals eaten on the cuff. Instead, Claiborne had hunted down fresh developments in the food world (a concept he was instrumental in inventing): new chefs and newly arrived ethnic cuisines; and, when the opportunity arose, he did actually cover the news in his field. For example, when Albert Stockli resigned as executive chef at Restaurant Associates in 1965 to open his own restaurant in Connecticut, Craig wrote about it, and the article was an early example of the sanctification of a celebrity chef in the major news media.

It was easy to miss the journalistic core of Claiborne's work, because he was so careful and clever about folding it into the epicurean format he'd invented for himself. In a given week, he would contribute a food feature, most often about an interesting home cook, to the Thursday women's page, euphemistically rebranded as "Food, Fashions, Family, Furnishings"—or in *Times*-speak, the four-F page—and, later on, as Family/Style.

On Friday, he would review restaurants, places he'd visited several times with three or four guests. These reviews were the reverse of impressionistic, filled with expert calls about ingredients and flavors, lapses in authenticity. To make things easier for the reader, he graded each place with from one to four stars. Very few restaurants got the maximum four stars, and the list barely changed from year to year, which was an accurate reflection of the placidity of the tiny world of elite food in New York from 1957 to 1971.

Also on Friday, there were brief recipes. And on Sunday, Craig would collaborate with the in-house photo studio on an illustrated recipe for the back pages of the *New York Times Magazine*.

This was a job description that fitted Craig to a T but nearly flattened me.

Toward the end of my tenure, I sat on a committee to discuss the future of Family/Style. Soon after, the section was parceled out into separate daily sections, with many journalists working on them. This redesign, which I favored, because it broadened food coverage and presented it more coherently, divided the food editor's superjob into slots for a principal restaurant critic, for other critics covering budget restaurants, for food reporters and a recipe writer.

I continued to perform all those functions while the redesign went forward. I did it all without training or contacts in the food community, and, worst of all, I had to operate in a depressed economy that hammered the luxury restaurants that were my basic "story."

A critic in any field needs lively new work to judge. If publishers stopped publishing books, book critics would have to stop writing reviews. This, of course, will never happen, even if and when all books are electronic. But in the New York restaurant world of the early 1970s, new restaurants of consequence rarely opened. Instead, several famous eateries were closing their doors. In my first few months at the *Times*, the city's most famous restaurant, Le Pavillon, served its last meal. So did the regal Café Chauveron, with its glittering array of copper pots, where I'd interviewed W. H. Auden for *Newsweek* in 1968, the winter following his sixtieth birthday. The Colony, an evolved speakeasy with fancy French food for a high-society clientele—pressed ducks and the like— also went out of business.

In journalistic terms, I didn't have much of a story, but that wasn't obvious to me or anyone else reading my pieces during my first few weeks at the *Times*, because I was able to make news all on my own.

Really, I didn't want to cause a commotion. I didn't suspect I was going to. Coming from *Newsweek*, which no one I knew ever read, and whose several million readers almost never raised a peep over anything I wrote, I did not dream that a short article about a Chinese restaurant in suburban New Jersey could spread frenzy throughout the tristate area and beyond.

But it did.

In my defense, I will stipulate that Craig and Charlotte made me do it. At the *purée mongole* lunch on my first day at the paper, far more important than Craig's grandstanding about the cafeteria chef's heavy hand with bay leaf was his offhand announcement that he would be leaving the city for his East Hampton dacha without supplying copy for that week's Thursday food feature. It was Monday. There was no time to get to know my staff or plan my debut article with my editor.

Craig wished me well, with a smile I can be excused for thinking faintly malicious, and Charlotte sent me off to personnel to become a salad handler and then to walk through an obligatory tour of the *Times* building for new hires.

What should have been an unchallenging bit of institutional tourism—a swing through the newsroom, a look at the acre of linotype machines that filled an entire floor of 229 West Forty-third Street and the presses in the basement—turned into a distracted, panicked perambulation during which I occasionally interrupted the tour leader's spiel to transact real business on the fly with the photo department or the Family/Style copy desk. Eventually, I found my way to the food news department, introduced myself to my very curious staff, and gave Jean Hewitt the recipe she would have to test under exigent circumstances, which included shopping for hoisin sauce in Chinatown.

For my first article as food editor, I chose the tryout piece I'd written about a Chinese restaurant tucked into a filling station on Route 1 in New Jersey, five miles north of Princeton. A Kitchen was a thirty-two-seat dining room attached to Sam's BP Gas Station. There was no Sam in sight, but instead Alex and Anna Shen filled you up with regular for thirty-one cents a gallon and also served "celestial banquets" to clued-in Rutgers and Princeton faculty members.

One of them, the sinologist John Schrecker, had stumbled on the place with his wife, Ellen, and discovered that the Shens served much more than the hamburgers, chop suey and chow mein on their regular menu. They were ambitious and authentic practitioners of "the same northern and Sichuanese dishes that have been appearing in New York City restaurants over the last few years," I wrote.

John and Ellen had for some time been introducing me to this exciting food as it emerged, elusively and without fanfare, in Chinese restaurants ostensibly devoted to the Cantonese dishes that had, until the late 1960s, been the only form of Chinese cooking available in America. But with the reform of racially restrictive immigration laws, non-Cantonese Chinese had begun trickling into the country, bringing the foods of their native regions with them. This new wave of Chinese immigrants often arrived on student visas from Taiwan, more educated and self-confident than the Cantonese laborers who had preceded them to work on the railways in the nineteenth century. Craig Claiborne had already noticed what was happening.

David Keh was the epitome of this trend. Born in Anhui Province, in eastern China, he had moved with his family to Taiwan after the Chinese revolution. From there, he came to America in 1964 to study at Seton Hall University, in New Jersey. He worked as a waiter at the Four Seas, which was one of the first, if not *the* first New York restaurant to feature non-Cantonese dishes, notably the spicy foods of Sichuan Province. By the late 1960s, he had opened the first fully Sichuan restaurant in town, Szechuan Taste, near Chatham Square, then at the edge of Chinatown.

The Schreckers, who had discovered Sichuan food in Taipei during a study year there, followed the American career of their favorite Chinese cuisine avidly. In fact, they were eager to hunt down new restaurants run by recent immigrants who cooked authentic Chinese food of any style, instead of the Americanized and adulterated dishes so prevalent in Cantonese Chinatown. So when A Kitchen appeared almost at their doorstep on Route 1, they called me, a pal from their Harvard days, and invited me to join them at an extraordinary banquet.

This was the meal I ended up describing in the tryout piece that eventually ran in the *Times* on Thursday, May 13, 1971, under the headline "Drivers Who Stop Only for Gas Don't Know What They're Missing." Inset into that article was the announcement of my appointment in italic type:

Mr. Sokolov, who has reviewed books, covered cultural affairs and been a Paris correspondent for Newsweek magazine, takes over this week as food editor from Craig Claiborne. Mr. Claiborne is leaving The Times after more than 13 years to pursue his culinary interests independently.

"A Kitchen," I wrote, "is not just a kitchen, but, preposterous as it sounds, one of the most authentic and dazzling Chinese restaurants in the New York area."

My new readers hearkened. Fiercely. In the hope of tasting the Shens' unchastenedly hot Sichuan bean curd, their handmade dumplings and their genuine "Peking" sweet-and-sour pork, they called (201) 329-6896, called it again and again, and if they were lucky enough and persistent enough to get through and book a table, they crowded into the little dining room on Route 1 in a frenzy of food lust.

Jean tested the Shens' recipe for eggplant with shrimp, while I watched. With the suspicion I would come to know well over the ensuing months, she told me she thought the recipe called for too much oil—two cups for two medium eggplants—but relented when the dish came together just as I recalled it.

And I was launched.

When word of the crazed response to the piece got back to the *Times*, I was happy and relieved. Charlotte was relieved and, perhaps, happy. She was hard to read, in her nasal and affectless midwestern way. Most important, A. M. (Abe) Rosenthal, the paper's despotic executive editor, was happy, too, but he did remark that I might have waited a few weeks before sending up this first-magnitude flare. Maybe it would have been better to start off more quietly, Abe suggested. But at this point in our relationship, he had not decided if I was going to satisfy his only criterion for professional acceptability: Would I be good for the *Times*?

He still wasn't sure, for the most part, because he didn't know much about food. At our first meeting, the day he hired me, he'd said, "I have more trouble figuring out how we should cover food than I do about reporting on SALT."*

He did, however, confide his relief that "at least you're not a queer."

Although we shared an interest in women, Abe and I, at bottom, we were fatally unalike.

He was a tough, up-from-nowhere graduate of City College, no intellectual, a Cold Warrior who'd won a Pulitzer as a *Times* correspondent in Poland, a natural reporter. I had a fancy literary

---

* Strategic Arms Limitation Talks, the U.S.-Soviet negotiations begun in 1969 that led to the Anti-Ballistic Missile Treaty of 1972, and to a never-ratified nuclear-arms-reduction agreement in 1979.

education, almost zero interest in politics, and a deep suspicion of the basic premises of the Cold War. He spotted me immediately as a dubious prospect. I knew he and I would never understand each other, especially after he told me that my beat was one of the few areas in the paper that made readers feel good about their lives.

Negative critics barely existed at the *Times*. The conservative art critic Hilton Kramer, then the cultural editor of the paper, was a very articulate, well-informed opponent of far-out trends in the visual arts. John Simon, acerb and mandarin, appeared as a free-lance naysayer sometimes in the Sunday paper. But the basic tone of *Times* criticism was middlebrow and allrightnik. And that was fine with Abe. He wasn't running the *Partisan Review* or *Dissent*. And he would never have hired me if he'd suspected that my ambitions as a food critic would be just as anti-establishment and rhetorically flamboyant as those literary quarterlies.

I knew perfectly well that food news at the *New York Times* was an inappropriate perch for an intellectual child of the sixties with a scornful view of the New York food scene and an angry reaction to its class-bound standards. Even in the conventional critical departments, the *Times* had not welcomed critics who threatened received ideas or deployed irony. Instead the *Times* had fought the bad fight against abstract expressionism in its art columns long past the point where sniffing at Jackson Pollock made the sniffer (and his publisher) look ridiculous. This stultifying atmosphere still prevailed in 1971.

So in the ensuing months, I kept up a show of preserving the Claiborne paradigm. On Thursday, I interviewed glamorous cooks, usually well-heeled housewives with modestly original recipes and entertainment tips for my less glamorous readers. My restaurant reviews seemed to follow the reactive pattern of the past: a new place opened and I judged its dishes (too much bay leaf in the *purée mongole*), no radical principles on view. And since the *Times Magazine* had a backlog of many months of Claiborne recipe pages with expensive color art already shot for them, I was regularly forced to lie low in that area, limited to writing blurbs for dishes I'd never tasted.

As late as December 19, 1971, I was still working off these Claiborne pages. On that Sunday, I concocted a blurb for two pheasant recipes. One I had inherited from a Claiborne favorite, the painter Ed Giobbi; the other, which I stuck in, was adapted from Escoffier. By then, I was thoroughly fed up with being Craig's anonymous ghost for those leftover magazine pages. Giobbi's braised pheasant was an innocuous enough thing. But in an oblique and childish swipe, I added the "utterly simple" Escoffier pheasant as a contrast to Giobbi's, which, I wrote, "calls for more ingredients and more seasonings."

Did anyone, even Ed Giobbi, notice the barb? Years later at an Upper East Side party, Giobbi's wife, Elinor, cornered me in order to commiserate with me disingenuously about how unsuited I'd been for the *Times* job.

If I had caused her discomfort with my pheasant blurb, that must have been nothing compared to the embarrassment and fury I'd caused Tricia Nixon, the elder daughter of the president, in my first few days as food editor.

On June 1, a Tuesday when I would have been preparing some routine interview with a cook for my normal Thursday feature, the White House held a press conference to announce its plans for an immense cake for Tricia's upcoming wedding to Edward Cox. The White House chef, Henry Haller, and its pastry chef, Heinz Bender, had developed a 350-pound, six-foot-tall, six-tiered lemon-flavored pound cake based on a recipe from the bride's mother. They also handed out a reduced version of the giant wedding cake recipe for home cooks to bake in their own kitchens.

My response was swift and lethal. I saw myself as the nation's designated palate, and I thought I ought to taste the cake the White House was proposing for the nation's domestic ovens. The *Times* would bake the home-cook version of that cake.

I turned the recipe over to Jean Hewitt, and she sprang into action. As she'd predicted after one look at the handout, it didn't work. The single-layer "cake" erupted from its pan all over her immaculate Garland oven.

I tried a spoonful and retreated to my typewriter. With the mighty web presses waiting to thunder below, I knocked out an account of the debacle. It ran the next morning, next to the Associated Press article about the White House press conference that included the hapless recipe, under the headline "Warning! It May Not Work."

As if this weren't a rude enough awakening for the White House, some staffers may have happened to read early editions of the *Times* in which two accidentally (?) reversed linotype slugs in the *Times* version of the AP recipe story stated that the cake "will have the initials of the President's daughter and her bridegroom, Edward Finch white, decorated with blown Cox, and will be iced in sugar orchids, white roses and pink-tinged cherry blossoms." The error was emended for later editions to the correct text : ". . . her bridegroom, Edward Finch Cox, and will be iced in white decorated with blown sugar orchids."*

Few people actually noticed this howler, but my article had a

---

* The linotype process, which was then used to print the *Times*, created lines of type— "slugs"—from molten metal. The slugs, all of uniform length, were then assembled into columns and locked into forms in a stack that reproduced the original text, but this worked only if the slugs were stacked in the right order. Somehow two slugs in the *Times*/AP article got stacked in reverse, with this result:

"white, decorated with blown
Cox, and will be iced in"
Instead of the intended:
"Cox, and will be iced in
white, decorated with blown."

wider impact. It was a cheap shot heard round the world. It certainly knocked the whisk out of Heinz Bender's hand.

My article came out on a Wednesday. Within minutes, food reporters from all sides were clamoring for quotes from me. I walked into Charlotte's little glassed-in office to find out what we'd do for the Thursday paper.

"Nothing," she said. "Today, we let everyone else scramble and make fools of themselves. Tomorrow, we jump back in. We're playing newspaper."

It was just as the lady said. On Thursday, June 3, we stepped back and let UPI, the wire service, carry our water. The official news was that Chef Bender, under huge pressure, had agreed to try the handout recipe himself but had refused requests from a horde of newsmen, including me, to watch. Mrs. Nixon's press secretary, Constance Stuart, was predictably indignant and stood by the recipe, but there was slippage in her defense. She conceded to UPI that the recipe should have called for a mixer instead of a blender. For his part, farther down in the article, Bender revealed that his recipe had neglected to mention the need to affix a brown paper collar around the pan to prevent the batter from overflowing as it baked.

For the same article, in what may have been an attempt to discredit me by eliciting a negative reaction to my article from my more famous predecessor, UPI interviewed Craig Claiborne. The reporter must have read the recipe to him, and then, to my great pleasure, Claiborne opined, "I've seen a lot of bizarre recipes, and I must conclude from this one that obviously the White House means whole eggs and not egg whites in the second step of the recipe." Then the old snake coiled back and let us have it: "But I shouldn't comment because I haven't tried the recipe—I haven't seen it printed because I no longer read newspapers."

On the third day, it was our turn again:

They tried to fix it up with brown paper collars, with longer heating times and changes of ingredients.

But after a hectic night and day session in Washington, during which both the White House kitchen staff and food writers for Washington newspapers announced a host of new recipes for the scaled-down recipe of Tricia Nixon's wedding cake, which flopped earlier this week in the test kitchen of The New York Times, the final version issued by the White House failed. Just like its predecessors.

It did not overflow the pan this time, or mess up The Times's oven. But it did not cook through, after 70 minutes of baking, and it was like porridge at the center.

The article goes on to describe various other fumbles and errors: corrections of mistakes in the recipe that accompanied the first UPI article, the discovery by Jean Hewitt that the quantities specified in both versions of the White House recipe gave improbable quantities for baking powder; this discrepancy would have helped explain why the batter had erupted in our kitchen. But the White House, our article went on to say, stood by its original quantities, while, nonetheless, increasing the height of the brown paper collar from two to three inches.

All these revisions kept Jean Hewitt very busy through Thursday, baking each new version of the cake, as each emended recipe emerged from the harried Washington kitchen. The final White House text, when cooked at the *Times,* "shook like jelly but tasted like a very soft French lemon soufflé," I wrote in an article that appeared on Friday, June 4.

"At the other end of The Times's kitchen," I continued, "was a very large mixing bowl brimming with nearly 100 egg yolks left from two days of trying to keep up with the evolution of Tricia's cake."

This was actually my second chance that spring to skewer the Nixon image in the *Times*. In late May, I'd been sent down to Austin, Texas, to cover the mammoth barbecue at the inauguration of the Lyndon Baines Johnson presidential library. I was one of at least five *Times* men and women covering this nonevent. There was a man from the Washington bureau, another from the national desk, the architecture critic Ada Louise Huxtable and Nan Robertson from women's news, ostensibly because of the fashion angle—or perhaps just because it was a major social event.

I devoted most of my space to enumerating the huge quantities of finger-lickin' fixins: eighteen hundred pounds of brisket, fifteen hundred pounds of ribs, a half ton each of ranch beans, potato salad and cole slaw for four thousand guests. One of them was Tricky Dick, whom I'd been taught to loathe at Mother's knee during the McCarthy era.

Mother had brainwashed me with Nixonophobia. In 1951, she introduced California congresswoman Helen Gahagan Douglas at a meeting of the Detroit chapter of the National Council of Jewish Women. Douglas had just been defeated by Nixon in an outstandingly ugly senatorial election in California. Nixon's campaign had smeared her as a Communist. Douglas invented the nickname Tricky Dick for him and smeared his supporters, in turn, as Blackshirts, still a familiar code word then for fascists. Mother practiced her speech hundreds of times at home. Eavesdropping, I memorized it without trying and imbibed its anti-Nixon attitude like an aural vaccine that would last me for life.

In 1953, when I was in Washington for my second year at the National Spelling Bee, I declined to join the other contestants on a tour that included the Capitol, because I'd seen all of the sights the year before and really wanted to hang out at the spelling bee press office in the Willard Hotel. A couple of reporters were whiling away the afternoon there when I walked in.

"Why haven't you gone with the other kids?" one of them asked me. Vice President Nixon was going to welcome them to the Capitol. Didn't I know that?

"I'm a Democrat," I retorted.

At that, the other reporter, an AP man, got up and went straight to the telex machine on the far wall. Down he sat and typed in two paragraphs about the eleven-year-old spelling bee contestant from Detroit who was refusing to meet with the vice president.

" 'I'm a Democrat,' the lad explained."

Other boys might have enjoyed the sudden national publicity, having their words sent out on the AP wire instants after they'd uttered them. Boys like that went into politics or show business. To me, the excitement was in the process I'd just observed. Oh sure, I got a chuckle out of taking a poke at Nixon. But what I loved much more and with an almost genetic affinity was the amplification of the poke. I'd just witnessed the creation of news, and I was hooked. A hack was born.

Twenty years later in Austin, I was living the life whose flavor I'd faintly sniffed in the Willard. But I hadn't lost my distaste for Nixon. And there he was, on the Saturday morning of the dedication, in a hideous aqua sharkskin suit, about to receive the LBJ library for the nation, and he was standing *ten feet in front of me*!

Security at a VIP event in those days was a lot lighter than the routine TSA checks at airports are today. There were no metal detectors, no pat-downs. All I'd needed to get into the library grounds that day was a press credential, which did not have my picture on it. I did not have a state-issued picture ID. Nobody did. So hundreds of reporters had ambled through the gates flashing pieces of paper, and that was that. I hadn't thought about it until I saw the president on the other side of a rope.

Then came the evil thought: Someone could easily have strolled in here with a pistol. I moved toward the rope. Tall men with little medals in their lapels loomed on all sides. I sidled casually into a gap between two of them, right up against the rope. Anyone could have done that. Nixon walked by, almost close enough to touch. Or shoot.

I worked some anti-Nixon potshots into my otherwise quite neutral piece. Readers learned that President Nixon had not stayed for the meal and had insisted on taking some barbecue with him on Air Force One, to nosh on, but only after his slow-moving entourage had kept the other four thousand guests waiting for lunch, while the pit mistress fumed like wet hickory.

With the end of summer, the opportunities for stunts stopped offering themselves, and the post-Claibornian routine took over my life, like a slow dance to bad music. The slim crop of new restaurants was slim indeed. La Chaumière, a modest French bistro in the Village, received no stars and a stiff, sniffy review.

There didn't seem much point in filling the Friday restaurant space with shrill warnings against such losers. I couldn't help hearing in my mind the voice of *Newsweek*'s cultural editor, Jack Kroll, explaining to me when I was a summer trainee in 1965 why the magazine didn't run a lot of pans of books by unheralded authors: "You're basically saying to the poor schmuck reader out there in Indiana: Here's a book by somebody you've never heard of and you know what? It stinks." So I began revisiting well-known restaurants, and if they didn't exactly stink, these Old Faithfuls didn't exactly make you excited about dining in them, or reading a half-hearted positive review reminding you that they existed.

On the same day I pasted La Chaumière, I gave two stars to El Parador, then the city's acknowledged leader in Mexican cuisine. The great migration of Mexicans to New York was still years off. Mexican ingredients were available only at one specialty store on West Fourteenth Street, Casa Moneo. So if you had been to Mexico or even San Antonio, you knew that El Parador was a provincial, if polite, outpost of real Mexican food. But it was one thing to know that and another to say it in the *Times*.

Three weeks later, I went to Pearl's, in midtown, and noted that "standards . . . have slipped." More to the point, Pearl's, I said, was "the perfect Chinese restaurant for people who don't really like Chinese restaurants," laying the groundwork for the most sensational reviews and features I would write at the *Times*. I also observed that Pearl's, with its prettifying rendition of Cantonese food, was "not part of the revolution in authentic Chinese cooking now in process in this city."

I did find one old favorite I liked a lot: the formal, vaguely Belgian Quo Vadis, on the Upper East Side. It kept its four stars and got a pat on the shoulder for its *filet de sole Dieppoise*, an elaborately garnished classic out of the as-yet-unrevised *Larousse gastronomique*. But Nanni's, recommended to me for its pasta by a well-heeled gourmet and member of many eating societies, flunked out in the meat part of the menu with an attempt at liver in the Venetian manner: "strips of the kind of gristly liver that have turned generations of children off the meat."

I ventured into Serendipity, the campy coffee shop and ice cream parlor near Bloomingdale's, to see how it was accommodating the new vegetarian trend under its Tiffany dome lamps. But what caught my taste buds was Serendipity's most flamboyant dessert: "the completely unredeemable self-treater will order apricot smush, a 'cold drink' in the same sense that Raquel Welch is a 'young woman.' It is a bracing bath of apricot essence, voluptuous and excessive."

You will have gathered that I was not happy with the mediocre gastronomic outback I found myself in, or with the treadmill built by Craig on which I was obliged to disport myself. But there wasn't much I could do to get the *Times* to change the basic formula Craig had worked with so successfully.

I did manage to persuade Abe Rosenthal to let me drop the Friday recipe feature and fold its space into the restaurant reviews. But he wouldn't let me drop the stars. I argued that attaching stars to a review cheapened it. None of the other critics were saddled with stars. Their readers couldn't just scan a set of graphic symbols before deciding whether to read the actual article.

He did, however, let me add another symbol: a triangle, the equivalent of Michelin's knife and fork, for ambience. I persuaded him that stars weren't enough: a place could have wonderful food with bad service and comfortless surroundings or it could be very pretty but have lousy food. It was the second case that I was really thinking about, because it allowed me to pinpoint an attack on that flower-bedizened, gastronomically overrated watering hole of the garment industry, La Grenouille.

Part of my covert plan to overthrow established order in the New York restaurant world was to knock La Grenouille off its plinth. And so I did, from four to two stars. But I also gave it a mingy two triangles for ambience, noting the way waiters called out to one another over the ostentatious flower arrangements amid a general decline in chic. Tables were so crowded together that people were almost sitting in one another's laps. But the real deficiency was on the plates: canned-tasting peas and a signature first course of clams in white wine I mocked as too humdrum for a top restaurant.

I knew this review would cause shock and awe. Important New Yorkers had a lot invested in their status as regulars at the Frog Pond, as La Grenouille was known in the pages of *Women's Wear Daily*. That trade paper responded to me with a special issue defending its favorite luncheonette.

La Grenouille survived my attack and improved over the years, outlasting all its rivals from the 1970s to become a justifiably beloved refuge of old-style elegance, the kind of place where *New York*'s perspicacious critic Adam Platt took his mother for a nostalgic meal in 2011.

Less sensational but more fundamentally influential was my review of Lutèce; I raised it out of the limbo of three stars to the golden summit of four.

It was clear to anyone with basic experience of great French food in restaurants in France that on merit alone Lutèce stood well above the other high-luxe New York French restaurants. But it was not part of the old-boy network of Le Pavillon clones, the *quenelles*-mongers who vied for the same high-society clientele.

Lutèce was different. Alone among its rivals, it felt like a real French restaurant, with topflight dishes you might have found in France and an unsnobbish atmosphere that also reminded me of my time in the *Newsweek* Paris bureau. One of my reasons for taking the *Times* job had been to give Lutèce its rightful fourth star. I bided my time, following Rosenthal's advice not to play all my trumps right off the bat. So nearly a year after I became restaurant critic, on January 14, 1972, Lutèce's two Andrés, Soltner the chef and Surmain the owner, awoke to unexpected but well-deserved fame and fortune.

On the strength of this accolade, Lutèce was launched for the next thirty years as the top restaurant in the United States. The combination of André Soltner's talent with the authority of the *New York Times* made this happen. But I was the one who made the connection, and within a year my rebel's judgment had won over the most grudging acolytes of the old order.

Ironically, the rise of Lutèce, which symbolized the final ascendance of authentic haute cuisine in America, coincided with the beginning of the end of Escoffierian haute cuisine in France and of France's domination of fine dining in the world at large. I got a glimmer of this future just a few months after the Lutèce review, in Paris just before Easter.

I got off the plane with no thought of discovering anything more than a minor shifting of the way things had been in the glacially advancing world of French cuisine when I'd left the *Newsweek* bureau in 1967. Nothing I'd read in the food press had prepared me for the upheaval that was finally bringing radical change to French food after the paralysis of the Depression, the tragedy of the war, and twenty-five years of postwar recovery.

This ferment was not, in fact, what you were likely to hear about in Paris, even from most resident gastronomes. I had arranged to have dinner my first night in town with John and Karen Hess, he a *Times* correspondent and future *Times* restaurant critic, she a notoriously precise cook and, later, an eminent food historian. John had been called away to cover the latest atrocity in Northern Ireland; so I ate alone with Karen at Chez Denis, an aggressively traditional small restaurant of the most refined sort. It might have been 1960.

I told Karen my plan to eat at a three-star restaurant outside Lyon run by Paul Bocuse, whom I'd heard about in 1967; my bureau chief, Joel Blocker, had proposed him unsuccessfully for what would have been an extremely prescient *Newsweek* cover story on young French chefs. Since then, Bocuse's restaurant, named after himself, had risen from two stars to three in the Michelin guide. Even I knew that. Karen Hess, however, evinced no interest whatever in Bocuse or my trip. Despite her obsession with food, she, like most Parisians, had not yet realized she was living in the middle of a moment of historic change in French cuisine.

I did find accurate guidance by reconnecting with Jack Nisberg, an American expat photographer who really did know what was cooking in the French food world. Jack had settled in Paris after World War II, studying photography on the GI Bill. He spoke hysterically ungrammatical but very fluent and vernacular French with a Chicago accent, and he understood the French character like no other American I ever met. I once saw Jack charm a crowd of Parisians packed onto a rush-hour Métro platform into posing for several takes of a picture. He wore florid sports shirts with no tie, which embarrassed Joel Blocker. And he wasn't a very good photographer. One of the bureau reporters liked to say that Jack took snapshots, not photographs. But he was truly serious about the art of photography. His idol was the American surrealist Man Ray; Jack had a small collection of his prints. And he was very good company.

Jack was happy to go to Bocuse with me, but before we left, he pressed me to book a table at a little place called Le Pot au Feu, in a gritty Paris suburb, Asnières, where another young chef, Michel Guérard, was creating a sensation with radically simplified versions of traditional food.

On the train to Lyon, I picked up a copy of the regional edition of the newsweekly *L'Express*, which some other passenger had left behind on my seat. It had Bocuse on the cover in his tall white toque. The article hailed him as the *chef de file*, the leader, of a revolutionary moment in French culinary history. It had all started in another Rhône Valley town, Vienne, in the kitchen of Fernand Point, where Bocuse, Guérard and the brothers Jean and Pierre Troisgros, now flourishing in Roanne, had apprenticed and learned from Point about what looked like plain cooking but turned out to be a deconstruction and rehabilitation of the entire tradition and practice of cooking.

Thus instructed, I dined at Bocuse with Jack. The next morning, I became the very first of dozens of Anglophone journalists to be taken by the great man for a tour of the Lyon markets, where he performed a sort of primordial locavore shopping tour at dawn. Then I went on with him for a midmorning plat du jour at his favorite little hole-in-the-wall, the kind of bar-bistro known locally as a *bouchon*.

Back in Paris, I sat in the tiny dining area of Le Pot au Feu for a meal of staggering flavors concealed in dishes of deceptive informality. At another lunch, I ate old-fashioned dishes at Alain Senderens's L'Archestrate. Some of them, like the fourteenth-century eel stew called *brouet d'anguille*, had been resuscitated from the earliest days of French cooking. Senderens also revived the intricate classic treatment of head cheese, *tête de veau en tortue*, and invented a subtle treatment of turnips in cider with a puree of celery on the side.

It was a spectacular week for an American gastronome, but for an American food journalist, it was the scoop of a lifetime.

On April 6, the Thursday after Easter, I did my best to describe the new world I'd blundered into, the "genteel revolution" soon to be known as the nouvelle cuisine. Paul Bocuse was the most theatrical of these Young Turks, as a person and in the kitchen. He served me a whole sea bass encased in puff pastry that looked like a scaly fish, with a tomato-tinged béarnaise sauce, what Escoffier called *sauce Choron*. But it was Michel Guérard's twenty-seat hole-in-the-wall that served the most forward-looking food.

A slice of *foie gras des Landes*, fresh foie gras from southwest France prepared in the restaurant, had arrived entirely unadorned, without aspic or truffle or even parsley. But this foie gras was of a smoothness and puissance to stand alone. For those who wanted something more varied as a first course, there was the *salade gourmande*—deeply green beans mixed with slices of truffle, fresh foie gras, chunks of artichoke bottom and an evanescent vinaigrette dressing.

MENU CLASSIQUE

Dodine de canard à l'ancienne pistachée et foie gras de canard maison
OU
Cassolette de Homard à l'armoricaine
OU
Quenelle de brochet aux écrevisses, sauce Nantua

Loup en croûte feuilletée, sauce Choron
(à partir de 2 convives)
OU
Fricassée de volaille de Bresse à la crème et aux morilles
OU
Filet de bœuf Rossini, sauce Périgueux
OU
Carré d'agneau «Côtes Premières» rôti à la fleur de thym

Sélection de fromages frais et affinés «Mère Richard»

Délices et gourmandises
Petits fours et chocolats   145

PAUL BOCUSE

Forty years after I wrote about Paul Bocuse for the *New York Times*, a picture of the same sea bass (*loup*) baked inside a fish-shaped pastry crust he served me adorns his restaurant's "classic" menu.

Guérard's *ris de veau Club des Cent* presented a sweetbread in one imposing lobe chastely topped with matchstick truffle slices and a clear, light brown sauce.

Some days chicken, some days duck came in a highly reduced sauce made from chicken stock, veal stock and wine vinegar. The light but intense sauces, the minimalist plating, the hyperdramatic focus on a single ingredient, the ironic refurbishing of cliché classics (fricassee, green bean salad)—all the elements of the new cuisine were there at Le Pot au Feu, the future ready to roll out and roar.

Back in New York, my food-alert readers barely stirred at this momentous news. Paris was far away. They would latch onto the nouvelle cuisine only when it came to their doorstep. But that wouldn't happen for several years. In 1972, in New York, the big news in food wasn't French; it was Chinese, because a revolution in Chinese food was happening right in New York City.

All of a sudden, it seemed, restaurants serving non-Cantonese food—the food of Sichuan, Fujian, Beijing and Shanghai—were popping up all over Manhattan. Word would spread among the food-alert and lines would form outside the newest hit address. Then the chef would decamp, quality would fall and we'd head for the next voguish installment of exotic dishes we'd never seen in Chinatown. It was almost as if some mad Chinese genius were making up one regional cuisine after another.

I can remember Julia Child puzzling over all the unfamiliar spicy Chinese food she was seeing. "We never had anything like it when we were over there during the war," she said to me.

She must have been too isolated in the U.S. intelligence community to experience the full range of local food. And like almost every other American after the Communist takeover of China in 1949, she couldn't travel in mainland China. To her and most other Americans who experienced it, the sudden explosion of "exotic"

Chinese eating places in our midst came as a surprise, a mystery, an ethnographic puzzle.

But there was a perfectly good explanation for it: a pivotal change in U.S. immigration law. That was the Hart-Celler Act, otherwise known, when it was known at all to the general public, as the Immigration and Nationality Act of 1965. This law revoked a forty-one-year-old immigration law that had strictly limited immigration by quotas that gave preference to applicants from the Western Hemisphere. In particular, the Hart-Celler Act abolished what was known as the principle of "Oriental exclusion," which had made it virtually impossible for Chinese to obtain U.S. immigrant status.

In the first ten years after Hart-Celler, the number of new immigrants doubled by comparison to the previous decade. Large numbers of them came from Asia and Latin America. And among this new wave of greenhorns were ambitious Chinese who invigorated the restaurant world of New York with regional specialties that made their fortune.

Of course, Hart-Celler did much more than improve the Manhattan restaurant scene. It literally changed the face of America. Arguably, along with Medicare, it was one of the two most important pieces of legislation of the postwar era. Yet few people are aware of it even now. In 1972, in the community of epicures, it hardly ever came up as a factor in the abruptly improved state of our gustatory happiness. We just wanted to know who the latest hot chef from China was.

In the days when a Chinese meal was nothing more than chop suey, chow mein, one from Column A and one from Column B, probably nobody in America ever stopped to think about who the chef behind the food was. But after more or less authentic Chinese food from several regions, notably Beijing and Sichuan, gained a serious following, Chinese chefs emerged as figures of the same importance as French chefs—but the Chinese chefs were much more elusive.

They were the subject of constant speculation by Chinese restaurant buffs. Few of them spoke English, the best had done their training on the Chinese mainland, and they hopped from restaurant to restaurant, leading their fans on a merry chase.

Take Wang Yun Ching of the Peking Restaurant on upper Broadway, who arrived in Manhattan after cooking at the Empress Restaurant in Washington, D.C., and used to give cooking demonstrations on local television. Suddenly, the ambitious new Szechuan Restaurant at Broadway and Ninety-fifth Street plucked him away from the capital and set him up on the Upper West Side.

Word got around. But just when lines began forming at the Szechuan as if it were showing first-run movies, Wang moved a block downtown to its new sister restaurant, the Peking. After a certain lag, the lines moved too, and made his lamb with scallions a word-of-mouth best seller.

With bushy eyebrows and a face that somewhat resembled Chou En-lai's, Mr. Wang had been a man in motion for most of his career. Born in a small town in Hunan Province, he began his nine-year apprenticeship in nearby Zhengzhou and moved through several other jobs until he reached the summit of his mainland career in the late 1940s at the Shao Yu Tien in Hankow. The restaurant specialized in wedding banquets and birthday or longevity parties.

Lou Hoy Yuen, the chef at Szechuan East (1540 Second Avenue at Eightieth Street), started work even earlier than Wang. He began his apprenticeship at the age of eight. An orphan, he never finished primary school, but practiced his trade at a succession of restaurants in Chengdu, Chongqing, Shanghai, Taiwan and Hong Kong. On a trip to Japan after the war, he met the Chinese painter Ta Chien, a gourmet who hired him as his personal chef and took him to Brazil. In Brazil, he met the shipping magnate C. Y. Tung, who invited him to work at the Four Seas on Maiden Lane in New York.

The Four Seas, now defunct, was, as I've already said, one of the earliest New York Chinese restaurants, if not the first, to serve the spicy dishes of Mr. Lou's native Sichuan Province. It was a haven for celebrities during the sixties— the architect I. M. Pei brought Jacqueline Kennedy; Danny Kaye ate there—and Uncle Lou, as he was known, was in the kitchen from 1963 to 1968. Then, just as Sichuan food began really coming into its own here, Uncle Lou left for Tokyo to escape friction with the staff at the Four Seas.

Meanwhile, David Keh, a waiter at the Four Seas, opened Szechuan Taste near Chatham Square, against the advice of many people who thought New York was not ready for an exclusively Sichuanese restaurant. Keh not only proved them wrong but subsequently had a hand (and a piece of the action) in many of the other Sichuan restaurants that sprang up around Manhattan after 1968, including the Szechuan on upper Broadway, where Wang had once worked. Keh floated uptown, and finally across town to Second Avenue for his biggest gamble of all, a Sichuanese restaurant on the East Side. He opened Szechuan East in 1972 on the site of a French restaurant, from which he inherited several hundred bottles of wine he couldn't use. And from Japan he brought back his old friend Uncle Lou, to be his chef.

Lou had a room over the restaurant where he napped between three and five in the afternoon, but the rest of the day he was in the kitchen, where he would make hot spicy shrimp or Sichuan beef in a few seconds of final cooking at his large wok. He would purposely temper the amount of oil and hot seasoning in his dishes "for Americans." But Uncle Lou's food struck most people as hot. He told me once that complete authenticity in Chinese cooking wasn't attainable outside China. Among other things, he had in mind one of the canonical eight great dishes of Chinese cuisine: camel hump.

In an ideal world, I would have been able to check that claim, not to mention various other details in the piece I wrote about mobile Chinese chefs. But I was mostly operating in the dark about Chinese gastronomy. The available books were a confusing mixture of intrinsically unreliable émigré recipes and memoirs. There was no Julia Child for the whole range of Chinese food. And even if there had been, the gap in cultural information between the United States of the 1970s and China in the area of food and food customs, not to mention history, was immensely greater than what Julia had needed to bridge a decade before.

My best sources were John and Ellen Schrecker, who themselves were primarily relying on the Sichuanese cook they had brought back from Taipei. By 1976, Ellen and John had published *Mrs. Chiang's Szechwan Cookbook* with her.

In 1971, I had the advantage of having eaten Mrs. Chiang's Sichuanese home cooking at the Schreckers', which gave me some basis for pontificating about the food at the new crop of restaurants. But with all those other dishes allegedly based on the traditions of Beijing, Shanghai and Fujian, I could rely only on a Westerner's palate and my experience with Cantonese food in the United States and London. This may not have been an entirely bad basis on which to judge unfamiliar dishes for an audience of newspaper readers with even less of a Chinese background than mine. Call it the blind leading the blind, if you wish, but for a first approximation, my reviews were openhearted descriptions that made sense to many readers. The way a dish at the pioneering Fujian restaurant Foo Joy, at the edge of Chinatown, struck me was likely to be similar to how it would affect readers operating with the same taste criteria and dining background I was deploying.

Anyway, I did what I could, riding a wave of public enthusiasm for this cascade of diverse new Chinese restaurants. I was no longer having to fill my review space on Friday with dutiful inspections of dreary new addresses and old favorites. The Hart-Celler Act had brought me a story. Then Washington played the China card again. In February 1972, President Nixon went to Beijing (it was still Peking in the *Times*), met with Mao and set in motion the open relations our two countries have today.

It was of special interest to me, of course, that Nixon ate at two Chinese banquets while he was in Beijing. The *Times* correspondent along for the historic trip, Max Frankel, won a Pulitzer Prize for his dispatches (and later became executive editor of the *Times*), but he found time to talk to me on the phone from China about the food at those meals, and I tried my best to put dishes I hadn't seen or tasted (or even heard of, in some cases) into some kind of context.

In the article I cobbled together from that phone call (a thrill in itself at the time), I quoted Max Frankel extensively. Up until I spoke to him, the banquets had been getting a bad press, those reports based mainly on the terse handout menus. But Max had eaten both meals and was emphatic that the dishes were spectacular—and that they were not what you'd see on typical American restaurant menus, because they were classic banquet dishes, made with exotica like sea slug, which was prized for its texture and rarity, or built around elegant conceits: a trio of recipes linked by a common ingredient—in one case, egg white.

Perhaps the most important point Max made should have been obvious: that Chinese cooks in China were aces at preparing the most elaborate and high-toned dishes from their millennial cuisine. At the level of a state banquet, at any rate, imperial gastronomy had survived twenty-five years of Marxism. And Max's description of the unfamiliar dishes made the implicit point that there was much more to Chinese food than what was on offer at traditional American Chinese restaurants.

This just added to the excitement among American gastronomes for the new wave of Chinese restaurants that were introducing whole cuisines hitherto unknown in our country.

This literal feeding frenzy reached its zenith just three months after Nixon's China trip, when Hunam opened in midtown Manhattan. Featuring the food of Hunan Province, among other things the birthplace of Mao, Hunam was a truly remarkable place, and not just because it offered New Yorkers a chance to taste a Chinese provincial cuisine never before served in their city. Hunam was also a superb restaurant with a very high standard of execution. There had never been anything quite like it. I was bowled over.

In a four-star review, I did my best to describe Hunam's remarkable dishes, which seemed to me like grander siblings of similar dishes I knew from the Sichuan repertory. For a first course, I recommended the hot-and-sour fish broth, which reminded me of ordinary hot-and-sour soup but, like so many of the Hunanese dishes, added an extra layer of elegance, in this case from fish stock and fish. The high point of a fine cold platter was raw shrimp in a subtle hot sauce that combined the tastes of Sichuan peppercorns and fresh coriander.

For a main course, one could choose honey ham, which consisted of two kinds of excellent Chinese ham with lotus nuts in a mildly sweet honey sauce. This very subdued and artful combination could be paired with a fiery lamb-and-scallion dish, a cousin of the Beijing dish with the same ingredients and the addition of a sauce as hot as any Sichuanese sauce, but taken one step further by additional seasonings.

Small, amazingly smooth and tender pieces of sea bass came in a hot sauce made with shrimp roe. Preserved duck was steamed on a bed of pork patties. Hot beef strips in yet another kind of hot sauce were served with dark green sprigs of cooked watercress.

If ever a phone actually did ring off the hook, it did so at Hunam on March 26, 1972, and every day thereafter, until the overwhelmed restaurant changed its number. No one had ever seen such a craze for a restaurant—any restaurant, not just a Chinese restaurant featuring food from a place almost none of the customers beating on its door had ever heard of before my review. Not until the Internet made it possible for millions of epicures all over the world to compete for seats at the world's finest restaurants was the Hunam madness substantially surpassed.

At first, I was delighted with my ability to mobilize crowds of gourmets and to reward a restaurant I truly admired. But I began to have second thoughts. Over the summer, angry letters complained about rude, rushed service, noise, crowding. Some of them also disagreed with me about the quality of the food. Others accused me of taking a bribe from Hunam's owners.

By November, the crowds were still coming, and Hunam's most impassioned customers had taken to showing up at four in the afternoon to eat their beef with watercress in peace. But the negative mail was also unrelenting. I decided to go back and see how Hunam was doing after six months of unexpected celebrity.

The food was still remarkable, at least what I was given. By then I was known to the staff. But the service and the setting, crowded with more tables than I remembered from my visits in February, were unfortunate, much degraded under the pressure to move diners in and out as rapidly as possible.

I wrote this in strong terms, but I also stood by my original judgment of the food. Perhaps this was a tactical error, but I could only review the food I was served. I felt compelled not to ignore a controversy I had done so much to foment, yet I now think that

I should have simply let it make its way, since it had been so auspiciously launched. A few weeks later, when I went to lunch, I couldn't get a bill from the waiter, and when I attempted to leave a large tip, I was physically restrained by the manager.

I never went back, but the suspicions about bribery never went away. When the charges surfaced in irresponsible gossip items, Hunam's owners apparently concluded that they had somehow misunderstood their proper obligation to me. They called my house to say they were in the neighborhood and wanted to stop by. I fled the house, but instructed my wife to accept nothing but food from them. A deputation duly arrived, carrying large bowls and trays of delicacies. But on their way out, one of the party thrust an envelope into Margaret's hand, saying, "It's for your children's education."

She ran after the visitors, having determined that the envelope contained a pile of hundred-dollar bills. They were on the point of driving off, but she managed to toss the envelope through an open window.

A month later, a UPS truck attempted to deliver two bicycles. It is not easy to refuse delivery of bulky items from a UPS driver who has already dragged them up your stoop, but we did.

In my increasingly chilly meetings with Abe Rosenthal, Hunam never came up, although I learned recently that he had eaten there and not much liked it. Clearly, however, Abe was unhappy with my performance, although he could not explain to me what was going wrong. From my point of view, I was doing fine: covering major trends in food in France and New York, visibly influencing public taste, attracting a faithful, even hysterically faithful audience.

Nevertheless, Rosenthal would not meet my gaze in the elevator. At a meeting with Charlotte Curtis, I asked what was wrong.

She essentially dodged the question, saying only that she and Abe thought maybe they had been crowding me and that I would do better if I followed my own instincts and stopped second-guessing what they wanted from me. This was well before the second Hunam piece; I proposed a piece about prison food with a list of other ideas during that meeting.

The prison piece appeared in the news pages over three successive days in June. For it, I ate the main meal of the day with inmates at three facilities, including the state maximum-security prison at Attica just a few months after several men had died there in an uprising that had begun as a food riot. Neither Abe nor Charlotte saw fit to react to the piece. Abe continued to turn away when we passed each other. By the fall, I'd begun to think it was time to look for other work, but I'd gotten used to the perks and prestige of my job, although I had more and more trouble taking it seriously.

One day, I told Charlotte I was considering a feature on zoo food.

"Start with dogs," she said. "The giraffes can come later."

I thought for a moment and saw the inevitable. "I guess I'll have to taste the stuff," I said. Charlotte smiled.

The next week, I brought my dog, Cleo, a four-year-old Saluki bitch, to work. We had shared a lot over the years, but this was to be our first joint meal. I went to a market near the *Times* and came back with a broad selection of commercial dog food. By then, my research had convinced me that most of the stuff, the mock stews and other prepared items meant to appeal to the tastes of human buyers—foods on which Americans spent $1.5 billion, four times more than they spent on baby food—were nutritionally unnecessary or worse. The veterinary scientists I interviewed for the piece were unanimous in their belief that ordinary dry dog food—kibble—was all a dog needed except for water.

The problem was that dogs who'd been exposed to human food tended to disdain kibble and wanted to be fed table scraps. Every dog owner already knew this, and most compromised with "wet" food from cans. So there was a destructive nutritional relationship between dogs and their masters and mistresses.

Dr. Albert Jonas, director of the animal care division of the Yale School of Medicine, concurred. His laboratories maintained anywhere from one hundred to two hundred dogs at any given time on dry food. But at home, Dr. Jonas admitted, his Cairn terrier often chomped into a plate of leftovers ("It's a pet. You know, the children . . ."). Like many lay dog owners, Dr. Jonas had allowed his dog to taste the poorly balanced but more delicious (for dogs as well as people) delights of human food.

What I decided I could contribute to this dilemma that flummoxed the elite of the veterinary world was the same gustatory judgment I applied to human food in restaurants. In order, therefore, to survey at least part of the vast current market in dog food, Cleo and I both sampled eleven kinds of dog food. Neither of us had eaten for sixteen hours prior to the experiment, but both of us had been previously corrupted by frequent exposure over long periods of time to a wide variety of meats and meat by-products.

Cleo point-blank refused to touch dry food—either Gaines Meal or Purina Dog Chow—although she was served it first. On the other hand, it was a matter of some peril to interrupt her ravenous feasting on the other nine varieties, which ran the gamut from raw ground beef chuck to chicken-flavored Prime to Milk-Bone biscuits to Top Choice chopped burger to liver-flavored Daily All-Breed dog food.

Cleo ate all the non-dry food (and the biscuits) with equal ardor and then took a brief nap. Meanwhile, I tasted very small amounts of the same foods, jotted down my reactions and attempted to rate the products' taste by assigning each a theoretically possible four stars, for dog food that could possibly be compared to ordinary human food, and so on down to no stars for muck "that would make you retch." The stars had nothing to do with nutrition.

My enthusiasm nowhere approached Cleo's, but I did approve the ground chuck and found the Milk-Bone tasty enough to consume two biscuits, the second spread with butter. Those two foods were the only ones to earn as many as three stars. Just below these in my estimation came chicken-flavored Prime, which actually bore a surprising resemblance to sweet Passover cake. There was no disagreement with Cleo about the two dry foods. But Purina Dog Chow was somewhat more palatable than Gaines Meal.

Sometimes an appealing stew odor belied a lack of taste. This was the case with Recipe's beef-and-egg dinner with vegetables and with Laddie Boy's chunks made with lamb. Both had a texture "nigh unto that of cold cream." The foods with the most unpleasant taste were the Top Choice chopped burger and Alpo horsemeat. One that could not be rated was liver-flavored Daily, an inexpensive homogenized food, brown-green in flavor and similar in effect to ipecac. It was not rated because "it was impossible to force the human subject to taste it. The dog, however, did like it."

Many readers took this article to be a parody of my regular function as food critic. They were not wrong. Some were offended at my disrespect for gastronomic connoisseurship; others got a laugh out of the thing. The article actually made its way into a serious anthology of dog literature, where I joined a pantheon of dog writers that included Rudyard Kipling and Albert Payson Terhune.

This was not a kind of immortality I had been seeking. I was doing my best to see that I emerged from the hurly-burly of the *Times* food department as an author of books. By the time the dog-food piece appeared, I was under contract with a *Times*-owned book company, Quadrangle, to produce an anthology of *Times* recipes eventually called *Great Recipes from The New York Times*.

Quadrangle had been acquired in part to provide an in-house publisher for books written by *Times* reporters. The plan was to deter these wage slaves from farming out books based on their work for the paper to outside book publishers. The shock of Craig Claiborne's having enriched himself via Harper & Row with *The New York Times Cookbook* had allegedly galvanized the New York Times Company into acquiring Quadrangle. And there was the hope that profits from book publishing would provide cash flow during the next newspaper strike.

I had waited a year before telling Charlotte Curtis that I wanted to assemble a cookbook from the recipes I was bringing to the paper, as well as some treasures gathered by my predecessors in food news that languished in the paste-up ledgers previously mined by Claiborne.

By early 1972, I had been pursued by several publishers, but the amiable Herbert Nagourney of Quadrangle made me an offer it was prudent not to refuse. It was, in fact, a very fine and competitive offer. At about the same time, I signed a contract with Judith Jones, Julia Child's editor, at Knopf, to write a book about classic French sauces, which was to be called *The Saucier's Apprentice*.

The idea had come to me when I was first at the *Times*. Green, ignorant, I was doing my best not to show it. And then I got invited to go on the TV quiz show *To Tell the Truth*. The other contestants and I all said we were the new food editor of the *New York Times*. And after we'd all tried to answer various food questions, the audience voted for the one whose answers had made him sound most authentically like a big-time newspaper food critic.

In the ten days before the show, I read my way through Escoffier's *Guide culinaire* and as much of the *Larousse gastronomique* as I could endure. Somehow I decided to memorize the sauces, which was fairly easy to do because, I noticed, they came in families. There's a book there, I told myself. I wasn't asked anything about sauces on the air, although I did manage to get myself unmasked as the real Raymond Sokolov. But I remembered about the mother sauces. When I mentioned the idea to Judith Jones, she, too, thought there was a book there.

My plan was to stay at the *Times* only until these two books were published, so that I would still be food editor when the time came to promote their sales. But by early 1973, my second anniversary was coming up. When I'd taken the job, I'd promised myself I would stay a maximum of three years, if things went well, and a minimum of two, if they didn't. I knew I couldn't wait much longer. Abe was not happy with me, for reasons best known to him. And I was not at all happy with my life as *Times* food editor. The week-in, week-out routine of reviewing mostly mediocre restaurants and interviewing mostly dreary cooks was becoming unbearable. From the outside, my job looked delightful, but to me it was a serial misery, especially the restaurant part of it.

One frigid evening in February 1973, I knew I had to move on. I had arranged to meet friends at a Vietnamese restaurant near Herald Square in Manhattan. Vietnamese food was still a novelty in New York, and I was looking forward to an interesting meal. But as I approached the restaurant, I heard sirens. Then I saw red, fire-engine red. And hoses. And police barriers. The restaurant was ablaze.

I needed to find my friends, but this was decades before cell phones could have solved my problem. And because of the sheer size of the police and fire department presence, it made no sense to stand there and wait for my friends to appear. I was on the east side of the conflagration. What if they were approaching from the west? We couldn't have seen each other through the smoky commotion.

The only thing I could do was walk around the very long block to the other side of the fire. And then back again every five or ten minutes, in the freezing cold.

A half hour later, we finally found each other, and fetched up nearby in an excellent new Indian restaurant, which lucked into a *Times* review only because of the very bad luck of its Vietnamese neighbor.

The next week, I sat with three friends for an hour and a half, waiting for dinner in a dreadful French-Japanese bistro that closed the day after my review appeared. And not long after that, the health department shut down a charming underground Haitian restaurant for attempting to operate without electricity. I had found this candlelit, one-woman enterprise to be a desirable place to sample Haitian cuisine as well as a plucky attempt at making it in New York on the slimmest of budgets. The health department shut the lady down because, without electricity, she couldn't heat dishwater to a high enough temperature to satisfy the law. But she couldn't afford electricity without staying in business long enough to earn the money to pay her Con Edison bill. By the time my review appeared, she had disappeared.

I got a call from Ed Klein, the foreign editor of *Newsweek*. He was about to leave on the first flight to China for U.S. journalists since the Nixon trip. Did I have any advice on where to eat? I suggested he try to visit an agricultural commune. Then he asked me if I was interested in returning to *Newsweek*'s Paris bureau. He needed to replace the bureau chief.

I said I was very interested. Ed told me he'd arrange it after he got back from China. Unfortunately, he didn't think to say anything to *Newsweek*'s chief of correspondents, Rod Gander, who hired someone else to fill the vacancy in Paris while Ed was away. Worse still, word got back to the *Times* that I'd been job hunting.

When Charlotte Curtis confronted me with the rumor, I couldn't deny it.

A few days later, one of Mr. Rosenthal's secretaries called, saying he wanted to see me. This was ominous. Normally, he communicated with me in regal memos ("I was not taken with your piece on . . ."). I went to see Charlotte first. She said Abe hadn't asked her to join us and she didn't choose to reveal what was going on, although she clearly had been briefed.

Abe's younger secretary waved me in: "He's expecting you."

There he was, a caricature of all the descriptions you may have read or photographs you may have seen of Abe: small and pudgy, bad skin, shirttails working their way out of his pants, an endearingly failed stab at a preppy look—bow tie and blue oxford-cloth shirt.

His expression was dark, but not scowling. Yet he was clearly troubled. Regret filled the room. Without admitting it, A. M. Rosenthal was taking care of a mistake. That would be me.

"This isn't working out," he said.

I waited for an explanation. Instead, he waffled: "Some people like what you do. Others loathe it. We will tell anyone who asks that you resigned for personal reasons. And the severance arrangement will be significantly more generous than the routine formula. I regret this a great deal. I've only done this twice before since I became managing editor."

He came to a halt, expectantly. It was my turn.

"I regret it, too. I was hoping to continue through the end of the year because of the Quadrangle book."

Abe looked confused. I explained about the anthology of *Times* recipes and how my departure would compromise the prospects of the book. He made a note to himself. That very afternoon, he called Herb Nagourney, trying, unsuccessfully, to quash the project. There seemed to be nothing more to say. He had canned me, without offering an explanation. I suppose I could have demanded some rationale, but I knew it would be pure waffle that couldn't be used in a lawsuit.

It turns out Abe assumed that I would do what the other misfortunates he'd fired had done. Determined to stay at the *Times*, they'd brought in the Newspaper Guild or a lawyer of their own and negotiated a new assignment in some dark corner of the paper. You couldn't be fired without cause at the *New York Times*, unless you let it happen.

I let it happen. And, as Rosenthal later told my friend Joseph Lelyveld, a career *Times* man and eventual executive editor, I was the only person he'd ever fired who had just shrugged and gone home.

Four

Upstairs in Front

So I was defrocked, denuded of power, of test kitchen, of company American Express card. Defooded.

Relief swept over me. I would never have to take food seriously again. I was out of that fat-slick cage for good. Relief at this realization helped to counter the painful truth that I'd been given the boot. Such complete failure, total rejection—I couldn't believe it had happened to me. But then I quickly did come to believe it—on that first Monday when I looked around after breakfast and wondered what to do with the rest of the day.

I'd always wanted to work from home, but this fantasy had included a full-time salary, benefits and an expense account from a major publication. Now I had the dream but nothing to support it or the nonworking wife and two children at St. Ann's School, at the other end of Brooklyn Heights from our comfortable duplex. Fortunately, the apartment, with a garden and a small office for me, cost almost nothing.

I would still have panicked if it hadn't been for the advance for *Great Recipes from The New York Times*, half of it still untouched in the bank and the other half owed after publication later in the year.

My *Times* severance would cover the summer, which we spent in our country place near Oneonta in central New York.

While Margaret prepared mentally for her first year at NYU law school in the fall, which she paid for with a federally guaranteed loan and which also had the side benefit of getting us all health insurance, I put out feelers for jobs in mainstream journalism and filled the weeks until my thirty-second birthday with writing a novel.

It was a short novel, eventually titled *Native Intelligence,* about a Peace Corps volunteer who flips out in a remote tribal village and dies. It evolved out of an anecdote I'd heard from my sister, Ada Jo Mann, who had been a Peace Corps volunteer with her husband, Tom, in Chad. The other impetus was a Quechua-English dictionary that my friend Peter Quint had brought me from a trip to Peru. I used it as the basis of the fake language in the novel.

Every morning I would retreat to the typewriter and bat out three thousand words, no more, no less. At the end of thirty days, I was done.

Never since have I been able to work with such discipline or so effectively. The shock of being fired overwhelmed any inhibitions I might have had about trying my hand at fiction. Also, I knew by mid-July that I'd be working as a fill-in writer at *Time* starting in August. My Harvard classmate Lance Morrow, a fixture there and a gifted essayist, had found me a spot in the non-news "back of the book." I would have preferred to return to *Newsweek,* but the editor, Osborn Elliott, wouldn't have me, because I'd made too much of a pest of myself as an anti-war activist for his taste. Thirty years later, by which time he'd decided I'd put away childish things as an arts editor at the *Wall Street Journal,* he joked across a dinner table about how when I'd worked for him, I'd been "a Communist."

I liked *Time.* For several weeks, I reported to the senior editor in charge of the non-arts half of the back of the book, a sardonic mensçh called Leon Jaroff. He was a talented science writer, and he had me writing about psychology and sex. The tone was serious, the standards high—much higher than my prejudiced image of Brand X, as we at *Newsweek* had referred to our senior rival in the newsweekly world.

At a certain point, I got transferred to the cultural side and wrote about television for Chris Porterfield, another smart gent. But the high point of my brief sojourn at the magazine was the cover story I wrote about plastic surgery under another enlightened senior editor, Larry Barrett.

The plastic surgery cover project had been knocking around for a while before it landed on me. If I recall correctly, there were already two full drafts that had failed to get into the magazine. One important problem had been the difficulty of finding an appropriate color picture to put on the cover that would exemplify the phenomenon of facial reconstruction without looking ghastly or ridiculous. Clearly shots of medically necessary plastic surgery—rebuilt elephant men and the like—were nonstarters. Cosmetic surgery could provide either images of successful procedures, which would have looked like any other pretty face, or unsuccessful operations—say, nose jobs with cavernous nostrils—which would have undermined the seriousness of the cover essay envisaged by the top editor, Henry Anatole Grunwald. (We met more as equals much later on, when, retired and half-blind from macular degeneration, he submitted to me, at the *Journal*, occasional columns on the decline of culture and civility.)

Henry was a phenomenon in American journalism, a polyglot and polymath, the son of a leading lyricist of Viennese operettas. The family had fled Hitler and settled in New York in 1940, when Henry was eighteen, too old to lose his accent but quick to find a toehold at *Time* as a copyboy while still a student at NYU.

Although I had little contact with Mr. Grunwald that summer

and fall, I got the impression that he was taking an interest in me. The regular change in my assignments, if nothing else, suggested that somebody on high was trying me out. The plastic surgery cover was pretty clearly meant to be my final exam, after which I might well be put on staff as a permanent employee.

I sensed this, but I found it difficult to take the project seriously. For me, plastic surgery was mostly a source of jokes about nose jobs and Brazilian babes who'd had their belly buttons removed. But *Time* had amassed a huge file that supported the theory that plastic surgery was a major social trend in America and therefore a topic worthy of the spotlight and the sanctification of a *Time* cover. I read and reread the files Larry Barrett had given me. Suppressing my misgivings, I had begun to write the article when Barrett told me about a piece of "luck." A potential cover picture was available. Elizabeth Taylor had made a film in which her character underwent plastic surgery. Paramount was offering us access to stills from *Ash Wednesday*, and I was going to fly out to Los Angeles to screen the film.

I did so the next day, catching an early plane and returning the same night on a redeye. In between, I cabbed to an office in Beverly Hills, where Bob Evans, already a Hollywood legend before he produced *Chinatown*, received me in his capacity as head of production for the studio. We were alone across a desk whose most memorable furnishing was a clear Plexiglas box filled with hundred-dollar bills.

After the briefest of chats, Evans led me through a door into an elegant little screening room. He left and the dreadful melodrama began. It was about a fiftyish wife who gets a full-body make-over on the q.t. in Switzerland so she can win back a wandering spouse—and combines the surgery with an affair of her own with Helmut Berger.

I sat through the thing, taking notes. Then I flew home, rewriting the lead of my cover story on the plane.

I sent a new draft to Barrett, who was not excited by it. Well, neither was I. But I could tell that the project was too important to get spiked. Mr. Grunwald was very committed. Then fate intervened.

A still from *Ash Wednesday* was selected, showing Taylor looking perfect, postop, in a hospital gown. But then Liz was hospitalized, for a malady by now long forgotten among the more than seventy other hospitalizations in her career. *Time* couldn't put a picture of Taylor on its cover playing a plastic surgery patient in the same week she'd turned into a real patient. The story was killed. My career at *Time* survived this reverse, but I was still not on the masthead by December, when I felt obliged to take a leave from the magazine in order to go on an eighteen-city book tour to promote *Great Recipes from The New York Times*. Before I left, I requested a meeting with Mr. Grunwald. I wanted him to evaluate my work for him so far. It was, he said, glib. But he'd be glad to see me in January.

Herb Nagourney went all out for my book. He sent me everywhere during the three weeks before Christmas 1973. I cooked Chinese tea-smoked duck on the hot plates of television morning shows all over the country. I took a twenty-mile cab ride to a snowbound suburban FM station outside Cleveland. I met dozens of food editors and got so bleary from the routine of daily flights and nonstop appointments that one morning in Seattle I convinced myself that a reporter with a French last name really was French; I proceeded to address her in her "native" language for five minutes before abruptly excusing myself to make a flight to Portland.

In Miami, a perky radio show hostess alleged that one of the recipes in the press release that had come with her review copy had a mistake in it. I was horrified to see that she was right. Fortunately, I had the presence of mind to look at the text of the recipe as it appeared in the book. It was correct. I was happy, but I was also impressed with this eagle-eyed woman who had detected a problem no one else in a dozen and a half cities had noticed. Sally Jessy Raphael eventually rocketed out of Key Biscayne to syndicated national talk shows on radio and television.

All in all, I had a great time promoting *Great Recipes*, but, despite a first printing of twenty thousand copies and my best efforts, the book didn't sell. So when I got home, I felt a bit sheepish handing in my expense sheets to Herb Nagourney. He merely shrugged and gave me the good news about the $75,000 book-club sale he'd just made to the Literary Guild. I would keep the lion's share of that—enough for the Sokolov family to live on for two years. I still felt bad about the failure of *Great Recipes* in bookstores.

After a year or so, however, I began to suspect that something good was happening with my book. Royalty checks kept coming in every six months, generated by sales of a reprint edition issued under the Evergreen imprint by an outfit called Barre Publishing. Given the low royalty rate for reprint editions, I ought to have calculated that my royalty checks implied brisk sales. I should have connected those numbers with occasional reports I got from friends about having seen my book for sale on remainder tables in bookstores, with an attractive blue cover. (The original Quadrangle edition had a garish, multicolored jacket.)

In 1983, a decade after *Great Recipes* was published, I was at the Frankfurt Book Fair, in an elevator at the swank InterContinental hotel, going to breakfast, when a man I didn't recognize greeted me by name and offered me a ride to the fairgrounds in his rented BMW.

"I hope you're satisfied with the way we've been selling your book," he said. I assured him I was very happy, but I actually had no idea which of my books he was talking about (there were three by then). At the fair, after making some discreet inquiries, I learned that my new best friend was Alan Mirken, the president of Crown Publishing, which owned Barre.

Even then, I didn't bother to get sales figures. But the truth will out. One day I got a call from a young man at Times Books, as Quadrangle had been renamed. "I've been assigned to do sales histories of all the books we've published since the *Times* acquired Quadrangle, and I'm happy to tell you that, although we never were able to move more than seventy-five hundred books, the Literary Guild and Barre between them have sold one hundred and ninety-two thousand copies."

I thanked him, reflecting that if his firm had sold 192,000 copies of my book at the original royalty rate of 15 percent on the jacket price of $9.95, I would not have spent the past decade grinding out freelance pieces for the likes of the University of Pennsylvania alumni magazine. I was still glad to hear how well I'd been doing behind my own back. But it was the book-club sale twenty years earlier that had mattered more. It set me free to be a writer on my own and to take advantage of some proposals that had come my way at about the same time.

During a book tour stopover for *Great Recipes* in Chicago, I'd run into Dick Takeuchi at the *Sun-Times*. He was the editor of their Sunday magazine, *Midwest,* and he needed a weekly food columnist.

More intriguing than that, I'd had a phone message from Alan Ternes, the editor of *Natural History* magazine, the monthly publication of the American Museum of Natural History. He, too, needed a food columnist, because so many of the museum's disciplines touched on food, including anthropology, botany and zoology.

I was good enough at math to count up the fees these two

recurring assignments would bring in. They added up to a modest but secure income.

I called *Time* and said I wasn't coming back.

At home in Brooklyn Heights, I set up an office on the second floor of our duplex apartment. Over the next five years, I typed my columns (the *Midwest* gig evaporated after a couple of years but other columns took its place, including a restaurant reviewing stint in *Cue* magazine, which migrated to *New York* magazine; I stayed with *Natural History* for twenty years) in this small room off an air shaft. When it came time to fill out the questionnaire from St. Ann's School for its parents' directory, in the space for "father's place of business" I put "upstairs in front," which made my dark, cramped office sound like a picturesque perch overlooking historic brownstones. The school left my "place of business" blank.

I was a very busy boy, juggling topical food columns for *Midwest* (one urged President Gerald Ford to emphasize his native Michigan regional cuisine at White House dinners: Great Lakes whitefish; Door County, Wisconsin, cherry pies; and Vernors ginger ale from Detroit) with book reviews for the Sunday edition of the *New York Times* (where I evolved into a once-a-month contributor to the "Nonfiction in Brief" section) and more ambitious features for glossies like the American Express magazine *Travel + Leisure*.

Abe Rosenthal would have been proud of my ability to multi-task. I will never forget the day I'd complained to him about being overworked and not being able to get going on long-range, non-deadline pieces.

"When I was a correspondent in India," he said, "I bought a notebook. Every time I heard something interesting, I'd start a new page about that subject in my notebook. When I learned something else about it, I'd add that to the appropriate page. Eventually, when enough material had accumulated on a page, I'd write an article. By the time my stint in India came to an end, I had ninety-three active pages in that notebook."

The thought of that notebook made me ill, but the lesson sank in. If he could turn his life into a journalism-generating machine, just by keeping track of it, so could I. The key for me, since I didn't have the constantly gaping maw of a newspaper waiting for my articles, was to arrange a set of reliable outlets in the form of regular columns. At the peak of my seven years of freelancing, which lasted until 1981, I was writing four monthly columns, with a book project simmering away on the side. The first of these, my novel *Native Intelligence,* was sold to Harper & Row in 1974, just as I was embarking on my new life of self-employment.

With that book off my desk, but still in the center of thinking about where my real future might lie—could I hope to write more fiction? was the rest of my ceaseless "typing" just piecework to support my new role as a literary artist?—I turned with reluctance to grinding through the intricate recipe testing and historical research for the book on classic French sauces I'd naively signed up to do for Knopf while still feeling buoyant and invincible in my catbird seat at the *Times.*

I'd been attracted to the project because it was a very good idea. I'd seen that the most elaborate and formal part of haute cuisine was organized into families of sauces based on a small number of highly refined and versatile basic, or mother, sauces from which the others derived. In a three-star kitchen, a saucier and his team would produce these intense essences, laboriously, day after day. Their rich tastes then gave the sauces derived from them a glorious profundity, which was one of the main things that separated a *grande luxe* establishment from a bistro. Bistros also offered diners tasty sauces, but nothing like what bathed the food at one of Michelin's three-star temples.

So the great sauces had always been beyond the reach of even most professionals in perfectly respectable French restaurant kitchens. It took an American amateur to see that those ethereal mother sauces (and all their progeny) could actually be made with relative ease by any home cook. Yes, a mother sauce was a big job, but once you had it, you could just freeze it in small quantities and melt it down at leisure. Voilà!

I thought the book would set me up as an expert on the most rarefied corner of French cooking. As Simone Beck, one of Julia Child's French collaborators on *Mastering the Art of French Cooking*, said later, no one, not even in France, had written anything like it. No one would be able to challenge my credentials in the kitchen ever after. Besides, I would be embarking on a great adventure, skimming my stockpot until its contents reduced to liquid gold. I would be democratizing the last bastion of professional cooking, and I could serve delicious three-star meals at home as easily as broiling a steak.

But now that contract hung over me, eating up my time, forcing me to spend money I didn't have on luxury ingredients for testing fancy classic recipes. I also had to buy the basic tools for making sauce bases in quantity, including an eighty-quart cast-aluminum stockpot, a butcher's cleaver and a fine-mesh chinois strainer.

I needed them in order to produce an industrial quantity of demi-glace, the *sauce mère*, or mother sauce, which is the basis of all the other brown sauces in the traditional French repertoire. There is also a mother white sauce and a mother fish sauce, but demi-glace is the Everest of the mother sauces. It keeps the cook at the stove for many hours, skimming and watching it reduce to a fraction of its original volume. So the efficient method was to produce demi-glace in the largest possible quantity feasible by a single person in a home kitchen.

In traditional French haute cuisine restaurants, where this

mother system evolved in the eighteenth century, larger staffs working for coolie wages could be deployed on such tasks. Antonin Carême, the most important chef of the early nineteenth century, perfected the original system in the kitchens of George IV, Talleyrand, Czar Alexander I and James de Rothschild, with huge staffs and princely budgets. Now home cooks could play his game, because they had freezer compartments.

My idea was to match up the assembly-line efficiency of the old sauce system with the preservation magic of the deep freeze. The recipe I developed for brown sauce stretched over six pages in twenty-six terse steps and required the better part of two days to complete. But once she had it, the home cook could blithely pour its five quarts of liquid mahogany into ice cube pans, freeze them and, the next morning, pop the cubes into plastic bags and keep them frozen in modular quantity, ready to be melted down almost instantaneously and then beefed up swiftly with other ingredients to make a classic sauce such as a bordelaise (demi-glace enhanced with a red-wine reduction and cubes of poached marrow).

Except for the ice cube stage, this was exactly how Carême and his culinary progeny operated. In *The Saucier's Apprentice,* I gave directions for twenty-five brown sauces, following recipes for their most unremittingly orthodox versions in the *Larousse gastronomique.* These "small or compound" brown sauces fitted neatly into a family tree, ranging from *africaine* to *poivrade,* plus two game sauces descended from *sauce poivrade,* which constituted a third generation, demi-glace's grandchildren. Similar families of plain, chicken and fish veloutés gave up their secrets in similar genealogies, as did the béchamels and the emulsified sauces, hollandaise and its cousins, the béarnaise group and the mayonnaise clan.

In this heady company, a sauce duxelles, sounding like the everyday mushroom mixture, and *sauce bigarade,* in name the orange sauce that has congealed around ten thousand bistro ducks, were elevated into the glistening and deep-voiced "gravies" that convert routine food ideas into great dishes in the classic style. Demi-glace was the reason.

To make it, I started with thirteen pounds of beef shin and thirteen pounds of veal shank on bones cut in three-inch lengths by a successfully cajoled butcher. But it was my job to strip the meat off the bones and cut it into two-inch cubes, which were strenuously browned in step 9. As for the bones, I put on goggles, stood the bones on end on a board, split them with a heavy cleaver and then splintered them further to offer the largest possible surface area for browning in the oven and for the subsequent extraction of their flavor during many hours of simmering in my very large pot.

It was large enough to hold a small child and straddled all four burners of my ancient gas range. When fully loaded with bones and meat and water, it could not be lifted. This pot took forty-five minutes to come to a boil. The heat it gave off blistered the Formica of the stovetop's backsplash.

While I waited, I picked bone splinters out of my clothes, and hoped I'd be done with this mess of a project before I went broke. I'd agreed to a mingy advance (half of which I wouldn't see until I handed in the finished manuscript) when I was earning a good wage at the *Times* and figured I could afford to do something I really wanted to do, for the joy of it. Now the joy part was muffled by night after night of testing elaborate dishes I'd picked from classic sources to go with the sauces.

The chapter on fish sauces was the roughest patch. For the mother fish sauce, I called a retailer in the old Fulton Fish Market and ordered twenty-five pounds of heads and bones.

"Are you a mink breeder?" he asked.

It sounded like a better career path than the one I'd taken. My sons have not forgotten those weeks of fish dinners, night after night.

The Saucier's Apprentice has never gone out of print, since 1976. The twentieth printing came in the mail in 2011. Students in professional cooking schools get it assigned for class. To me, it means more now as an early example of my future as a food historian. In addition to the utterly orthodox sauce recipes, the book starts with a historiographical essay on the French cookbook legacy, and it is filled with lovingly gathered tidbits from the food scene of the Parisian Gilded Age. I even invented a period dish to go with *sauce bordelaise,* because the obvious choice from the classic repertoire, *tournedos Rossini,* required fresh foie gras, which was then unavailable in the United States.

Since the composer Rossini may have actually invented the dish, I thought I could appropriately name my filet mignon recipe after another luminary of his world. Tournedos Rachel honors the great French actress, born Elisa Felix (1820–1858), by garnishing the steak with artichoke bottoms and marrow instead of the foie gras and the unaffordable black truffles of the original.*

So some of the recipes in *The Saucier's Apprentice* were original, but even they were modest variations on haute cuisine standards,

---

* I had in mind, as well, a fictional Rachel, a probably Jewish prostitute turned actress in Proust's *In Search of Lost Time. That* Rachel's name is part of an elaborate tangle of references: to the biblical heroine and to the historical actress of the same name.

Proust linked the fictional Rachel with his own life and with the contemporary Parisian opera scene when he had her aristocratic lover, the character Robert de Saint-Loup, refer to her as "Rachel, quand du Seigneur" (Rachel, when from the Lord). This was the first line of the popular aria from Fromental Halévy's opera *La Juive* (The Jewess).

This was not simply a throwaway cultural allusion for Proust. Halévy's daughter Geneviève married the composer Georges Bizet. Their son, Jacques, was pursued amorously by Proust at the Lycée Condorcet. After Georges Bizet died, Geneviève Halévy Bizet married a Rothschild-connected banker named Émile Straus and presided over an elegant salon, at which Proust was a frequent guest. He used Madame Straus as one of the models for the duchesse de Guermantes, the aunt of Proust's Rachel's Saint-Loup in *In Search of Lost Time.*

and the core of the book, the sauce recipes themselves, were as traditional as I could make them.

Ironically, I was devoting myself in Brooklyn in 1974 to a primer for the most conservative and elite possible form of French cooking, whereas in France, young chefs were turning their backs on Escoffier, and I had been the first English-speaking journalist to herald their revolution in 1972. But I had signed my contract before I'd encountered the nouvelle cuisine in France. So I soldiered on. Moreover, I believed that it was simply too early for an outsider to be writing about the radical upheaval going on in France. The burgeoning practical food historian in me was confident of the need for an analytical, reliable account of the central dogma of haute cuisine, its sauces.

It turned out to be laughable that I was worried about being overtaken by history. The original breakthroughs in French kitchens around 1970 did eventually spread around the world and provoke similar reforms and deconstructions of traditional cuisines, from Peru to the Philippines. Certainly, by the 1990s, the revolution I happened on chez Bocuse and Guérard had so completely prevailed that the term "nouvelle cuisine," coined by its first and foremost promoters, Henri Gault and Christian Millau, in their influential French restaurant guide, had acquired a period patina.

When I used it as a shorthand way of tagging the food at an inventive California restaurant in a letter to M. F. K. Fisher shortly before her death in 1992, the ever-acute chronicler of foodways from Sonoma to Dijon replied, "Nouvelle cuisine? Isn't it just the way we eat now?"

Yes, but along the way to that knowing dismissal lay twenty years of misunderstanding about nouvelle cuisine and its ripple effect in professional kitchens around the globe. The chefs marched ahead with an instinctive grasp of the dynamic process they were caught up in, even as it swept them forward. But all around them was confusion. Especially in North America, where the terms of the debate were fundamentally garbled in translation, the new cooking got hijacked by publicists and trend-riding journalists who floated various semitruths that gelled into orthodox explanations of complex change at the top of the food world.

Without meaning to mystify, two restaurateurs deeply devoted to the French past had completely bamboozled the public about its future.

Michel Guérard, the most gifted of the leaders of the nouvelle cuisine, wrote a best-selling diet book, *Cuisine minceur*, published in the United States in 1976. After his epoch-making Le Pot au Feu had been razed to widen a street, Guérard had followed his wife to a palatial spa in southwest France owned by her father. Guérard offered spa clients a modern, nouvelle cuisine–informed menu of slimming dishes, while serving regular gastronomes a calorie-insensitive carte of grand and brilliant creations that eventually appeared in his masterwork, the far less popular but far more important *Cuisine gourmande* (1977 in France, 1978 in English translation).

Guérard was undoubtedly sincere in believing that the lighter, less baroque dishes he served his fat-obsessed guests at Eugénie-les-Bains would make them thinner without depriving them of the delights of great cooking. He had clearly been won over to a fervor for health by his new wife, a lifelong purveyor of healthy regimens who said in an interview shortly after her marriage to Guérard, "We will not grow old and fat together."

Guérard, who had lost a lot of weight under pressure from his wife, found a way of linking their spa menus to his premarital work at Le Pot au Feu, which, along with many other innovations, replaced the flour-thickened brown sauces of yore with flourless and highly reduced *jus*. And in press accounts that accompanied *Cuisine minceur*, the notion of flourless sauces adopted from nou-

velle cuisine as the central instruments of Guérard's diet program crowded out nuance and contributed to the widespread and
mostly ineradicable misconception that nouvelle cuisine itself was
a dietary program, a three-star method for taking off pounds.

Although the new sauces were indeed flourless, it had never
been the case that the great kitchens of France, under Carême or
Escoffier or Point, bathed food in gluey brown gravies. It was true
that the demi-glace of Escoffier incorporated a very small amount
of flour in the form of roux, flour browned in butter before it was
whisked into a sauce. But this did not thicken a demi-glace in anything like the crude way that flour thickened the gravy on a hot
turkey sandwich in school cafeterias and greasy spoons all over
America in that era.

But it was that reflex confusion, between a subtle difference in
the practice of top-level French chefs and the blatant viscosity of
an American "classic" brown sauce, that misled U.S. readers of
reviews and other accounts in the press of *Cuisine minceur*.* Since
virtually none of them had ever eaten a nouvelle cuisine meal, it
was easy for them to conclude that Guérard and his confreres had
given up their bad old ways and converted to a fancy form of nutritional sanctimony.

Anyone who actually read *Cuisine minceur* could not have
put much stock in this (so to speak). In fact, it now seems totally
incredible that diet-obsessed Americans would have taken *Cuisine
minceur* seriously as a guide to weight reduction. No nutritional
breakdown of any dish is offered. Calories are neither counted nor
even mentioned, except in the titles of recipes like "low-calorie
mayonnaise," which is still caloric enough for Guérard to advise

---

* "It is Michel Guérard who is France's true pioneer of low-fat, high-pleasure cuisine,"
said *Newsweek*. "Joyful penitence for the overindulger," declared Gael Greene in *New York*
magazine. "An assault on the twin modern enemies of trenchermen: calories and choles-
terol," opined Joseph Wechsberg in the *New Yorker*.

using it sparingly. The first half of the book is a thoroughly conventional set of basic cooking instructions hardly different from what could have been found in any French culinary primer.

It is true that the preponderance of recipes that fill the second half of the book are on the lean and mean side. Sautéeing is suppressed in favor of poaching, but the poaching is done in chicken stock instead of water. Yes, the desserts are very fruit forward. Guérard recommends artificial sweetener to replace sugar. He chooses a soufflé that depends entirely on egg whites. But he just can't resist including directions for cream puff dough—yielding only enough *pâte à choux* for an individual portion.

To be fair, someone who turned to *Cuisine minceur* after a misspent life of three-martini meals, burgers and French fries, and apple pie à la mode would almost certainly lose weight if she stuck to Guérard's recipes religiously and gave up, as he demands, all alcohol. But *Cuisine minceur* is not a dietary method, and its recipes were not invented from the ground up to combine nutritional sobriety with gustatory interest. They are, almost all of them, standard dishes selected from the French repertory because they are low in fat, flour and sugar. Their real interest, however, is in their relationship to Guérard's overall practice as the most innovative of all the nouvelle cuisine chefs.

As in his nutritionally unbridled *Cuisine gourmande,* Guérard applies his culinary intelligence to vegetables. I mean he purees all manner of vegetables not normally treated that way, ending up with sharply focused flavors and pools of brilliant natural colors to brighten plated entrées. These purees of watercress and beets and spinach and green beans stood in, with daring minimalism, for the fussy garnishes of the Escoffier platter.

In *Cuisine minceur,* they are every bit as dramatic as they are in *Cuisine gourmande,* and Guérard could present them simply as low-calorie side dishes. But you can see still his "gourmande" intelligence at work in the recipe for watercress puree II, which includes lemon juice and a bit of crème fraîche for a slightly grander, more unctuous effect. (The same dish would appear in *Cuisine gourmande* a year later, with some butter and a far greater quantity of crème fraîche.)

These purees were called *purées mousses* in the original French, which carries nuances lost in the plainer English "puree," meaning something blenderized to perfect smoothness. In everyday French, though, *purée* (all by itself) could mean mashed potatoes (as would *mousseline*). So to my ear, the ever-metaphorical Guérard wanted his French readers to think of his Technicolor vegetable purees as glamorous cousins of mashed potatoes. Which, of course, they are.

Elsewhere in *Cuisine minceur*, he retreats even further from the diet book mode and into the improvisational full sun of nouvelle cuisine with a dish originally called *gratin de pommes du pays de Caux*. In Narcisse Chamberlain's English translation, this comes out as Normandy fruit and artichoke gratiné, which is perhaps too helpful. Guérard's title leaves out the artichoke as well as the fresh apricots, which are all parcooked and then baked in a custard. Undoubtedly, Guérard meant to surprise and amuse French readers (and the guests they served) with the unmentioned (and hitherto uncombined) ingredients.

When served, they would have been invisible or at least unrecognizable in the custard, until their tastes gave them away. They also added two extra textures—one more solid (the artichoke), the other softer (the apricot)—to that of the pure apple people were expecting to find in a dish they could see was not a gratin, because it had no layer of melted cheese on top. This "gratin" looked, in fact, like the rustic custard or fruit dessert called *clafoutis*.

What is "minceur" about this "gratin"? Guérard specifies nonfat dry milk—but also lists two whole eggs for the custard.

In *Cuisine gourmande*, the full panoply of Guérard's genius was on display: an entire chapter of foie gras recipes; a metaphorical carnival of frogs' leg Napoleons; a seafood stew (*navarin*) steamed over seaweed; beef cheeks à l'orange; beef in the manner of fish (*filet de boeuf en poisson*). This last dish involved butterflying an entire beef tenderloin, inserting truffle slices all over its interior to resemble fish scales, closing it up for roasting, then reopening it on a serving platter and putting a puff pastry fish head and fish tail at either end, to make a faux fish. There was also a sauce, truffle juice thickened with over a half pound (250 grams) of butter. Here was the real Guérard, a more fully achieved version of the genius of Le Pot au Feu. It was this Guérard who earned three stars in Michelin* in 1977 and won the general agreement of the cognoscenti that he was the outstanding French chef of his generation.

After *Cuisine gourmande* and cookbooks from other nouvelle cuisine chefs began appearing in English, American chefs and wannabes read those books and soon found ways to infiltrate their authors' kitchens in France, returning home to establish beachheads of modern innovation.

David Bouley prepared for his career as a New York star chef by enrolling in the Sorbonne and then "studying" at the feet of five of the new wave's A team: Paul Bocuse, Joël Robuchon, Roger Vergé, Frédy Girardet and the patissier Gaston Lenôtre. Returning home, he worked at top established restaurants until surfacing in Tribeca's first serious restaurant, Montrachet, in 1985, and then opening Bouley in 1987.

In a less obvious trajectory from French training to his own temple of post-nouvelle cuisine, Thomas Keller first knocked

* He had them still in 2011.

At the back, Thomas Keller at La Rive, near Catskill, New York, ca. 1981, with his employers, René and Paulette Macary, and the rest of the staff of this very French country inn

around the American restaurant world. Then he fetched up at a French-owned country inn in the woodsy hinterland of Catskill, New York. La Rive was a treasure of traditional French cooking for anyone who could find it. I remember it well, a rustic piece of France in the Hudson Valley. But I had no idea that an American was behind the scenes, imbibing tradition from his strict employers, René and Paulette Macary. Keller spent three years there, experimenting on his own with smoking and other old-fashioned farmhouse techniques. He wallowed in organ meats and might have continued on this path to retro, down-home *aubergisme,* if he had been able to buy La Rive. When he couldn't pry it loose from its owners, he decamped for France in 1983 and went straight to the top of the Parisian food scene, cooking in the most celebrated of traditional kitchens at Taillevent and at the cleverest of second-generation modern restaurants, Guy Savoy.

Back in New York, he practiced traditional French elegance at La Reserve and then spent time at the city's main colony of *nouvellisme,* Raphael. In 1987, Keller, like Bouley, moved downtown, where he showed his radical colors at Rakel, whose menu mixed French technique with native ingredients such as the jalapeño pepper. Rakel closed at the end of the eighties and Keller spent some years in the wilderness before ascending to the summit of the U.S. restaurant world in the undeniably French but thoroughly modern and original French Laundry, in the wine village of Yountville, California, in 1994.

So nouvelle cuisine eventually trickled across the Atlantic. Before long, it was taken for granted by a new generation of American chefs trained by those who had apprenticed in France. They and their customers had gotten the message, but I felt the message itself had never been properly articulated. In my *Natural History* column and elsewhere, I set out to tell its complex story and to "deconstruct" its essence.

On the technical level, all the original chefs in the movement agreed that flour-thickened sauces were an abomination, but their preference for sauces built around heavily reduced stocks or stocks thickened with cream or egg yolks or hollandaise sauce did not amount to a revolution. Neither did the new emphasis on fresh ingredients, al dente vegetables, and raw fish and meat. It was this ingredient-centered, health-conscious side of early nouvelle cuisine that understandably misled people into thinking that Guérard, Bocuse et al. were a bunch of health-food enthusiasts with good knife skills. Bocuse encouraged this confusion when he said his innovations were aimed at the new gourmet, a hypothetical diner consumed with a passion for great food but preoccupied as well with staying trim.

This was undoubtedly a shrewd insight into the upscale clientele of three-star restaurants, but even a cursory glance at the

THE FRENCH LAUNDRY

CHEF'S TASTING MENU | 30 MARCH 2012

"OYSTERS AND PEARLS"
*"Sabayon" of Pearl Tapioca with Island Creek Oysters
and White Sturgeon Caviar*

ROYAL OSSETRA CAVIAR
*Speck, Quail Egg, "Blini"
and Maple Syrup*
(50.00 supplement)

VELOUTÉ OF WHITE ASPARAGUS
Nantes Carrot, English Peas and Pickled Onions

MOULARD DUCK "FOIE GRAS AU TORCHON"
*Sour Michigan Cherries, Tokyo Turnips, Marcona Almonds
and Black Winter Truffle*
(30.00 supplement)

ATLANTIC STRIPED BASS "EN PERSILLADE"
*Three Bean Salad, Jingle Bell Peppers
and Dijon Mustard*

SWEET BUTTER-POACHED ALASKAN KING CRAB
*Hobbs' Bacon "en Feuille de Brick," Red Radish,
Romaine Lettuce and Hass Avocado "en Gelée"*

GEORGES BANK SEA SCALLOP "POÊLÉE"
*Bone Marrow "Pain Perdu," Green Asparagus, Cipollini Onion,
Watercress and Apricot-Riesling Emulsion*

LIBERTY FARM PEKIN DUCK
*Violet Artichokes, Cara Cara Orange,
Broccoli and "Sauce Hydromel"*

MARCHO FARM NATURE-FED VEAL
*"Ris de Veau," Tripe, Buckwheat "Annellini,"
Stinging Nettles and Green Garlic*

GRILLED BLACKMORE RANCH WAGYU
*Asian Pear, Celery, Pine Nuts, Mint
and Sweet & Sour Eggplant*
(100.00 supplement)

"BLEU D'AUVERGNE"
*Belgian Endive, Young Fennel,
Green Grapes and Red Walnut*

SIERRA BEAUTY APPLE SORBET
Toasted Oats and Ginger "Nuage"

"MARJOLAINE"
*Praline Mousse, "Dacquoise,"
and Roasted Banana Sherbet*

MEYER LEMON "PARFAIT"
*Oregon Huckleberries, Sicilian Pistachios
and Poppy Seed Ice Cream*

MIGNARDISES

PRIX FIXE 270.00 | SERVICE INCLUDED

6640 WASHINGTON STREET, YOUNTVILLE CA 94599 707.944.2380

ingredients actually served up by Bocuse and the other Young Turks should have convinced us all that the dietary claims blandly proffered in interviews by Bocuse and Alain Senderens, of L'Archestrate in Paris, were a soufflé of rationalization.

Guérard was an even greater, if sincere, contributor to the miasma of hygiene that befogged nouvelle cuisine in its period of maximum press attention.

Hidden behind this screen of contradictions and opportunistic rhetoric, nouvelle cuisine was actually something radically new that had sprung right out of the social fabric of postwar France. Young chefs had eliminated the formally garnished banquet platters of Escoffier (which were themselves simplifications of the grandly sculptural cuisine inherited from Carême and other classical nineteenth-century practitioners). In this cleansing of the repertory, these chefs were following not only the relatively inconspicuous and mild reforms of Escoffier but also the more trenchant and simplifying example of their mentor Fernand Point. They were, in fact, picking up a thread first spun in the period between the wars when the influential gastronomic writer Curnonsky had directed the attention of chefs like Point to the treasures of French regional cooking. In a series of blue booklets aimed at the new breed of gastronomically inclined motorists, Curnonsky not only recorded these local dishes but also insisted that they should reflect their ingredients, should not disguise the taste of the things from which they were cooked. Today this may seem like an obvious principle, but the extremely complex recipes of nineteenth-century haute cuisine were edible fantasies remote from the raw materials of the larder.

Opposite: An embarrassment of choices at the French Laundry, in Yountville, California. Will it be a tasting of classics like oysters and pearls or foie gras from the meat *dégustation* menu, or more intensely original treatments of peas and beets on the vegetarian roster? We ordered both in 2004.

And so, when Paul Bocuse prided himself on his *cuisine du marché* (market cooking) and took reporters like me with him to the market in Lyon to hunt for the best raw materials available on a particular day, he was showing his commitment to ingredients, to their intrinsic taste and quality, and to the resources of his own region. And by the time Bocuse and the other Young Turks had achieved national and international fame, they had gone further than Point.

By the mid-seventies, I had eaten in most of their restaurants. On a meal-by-meal basis, no clear picture of a unified direction had emerged. What, if anything, was the connection between Bocuse's gargantuan sea bass en croûte with a *sauce Choron* (béarnaise with tomato puree) and the black, unglamorous, juniper-infused thrush pâté at Troisgros?

Then I happened to compare the pictures in Point's posthumous *Ma gastronomie* (1969) with those in Guérard's *Cuisine gourmande* and still other photographs in Jean and Pierre Troisgros's *Cuisiniers à Roanne* (1977). Point's food looks radically simple alongside the platters depicted in the *Larousse gastronomique*, with their garnishes of turned vegetables and pastry boatlets, but with Point we are still in the world of the banquet, the world of the platter on which a suckling pig or a whole tart is presented to a tableful of people or a large family assembled for a dramatic occasion.

The younger chefs selected photographs of individual plates, with the food on them arranged meticulously to make a visual effect on its own. In their book, the brothers Troisgros credit their father as the source of the "custom of both presentation and service on each guest's individual plate—very large plates, which we were the first to use."

By now we have all encountered the nouvelle cuisine plate and its studied placement of sliced vegetables, arranged in circular or other geometric patterns. While it would be wrong to dispute that this new mode of decoration arose in France and quite naturally from trends emerging over decades, it is also the case that the full efflorescence of nouvelle cuisine was, to an important extent, an exotic bloom fertilized by new ideas, aesthetic and culinary, that traveled to France from abroad, in particular from Japan, and took root in traditionally xenophobic soil.

In the postwar era, exotic ingredients—the avocado, the mango and, before all others, the kiwi—arrived in France by jet. Meanwhile, French people traveled outside the mother country in unprecedented numbers. Bocuse himself jetted off so often to Japan that diners complained that the master was rarely at his own stove. Senderens abandoned his research in premodern French recipes to study Japanese cuisine.

The flow of ideas from Japan to France brought a highly developed food aesthetic—one based on delicate visual effects and achieved most often on individual plates—to young French chefs already predisposed to paint with food on the circular field of a plate. Nouvelle cuisine rapidly evolved into a feast for the eyes, *à la japonaise*. It also incorporated some of the basic ideas of Japanese cuisine itself, notably a predilection for raw ingredients, which fulfilled Curnonsky's notion of ingredient purity to perfection. A slice of raw scallop tasted, by definition, of nothing but the scallop itself.

The global success of this new mode of cooking is a fact of contemporary life, reinvigorating national and regional food traditions. It is to this global yet regional school of cookery that we in America now owe the so-called new American cuisine, which combines French principles of food preparation, Japanese plate decoration and regional, folkloric American ingredients.

On wings of chic, I wrote in *Natural History*, the new gospel soared over oceans and continents. Japanese chefs trained in

France reigned supreme in Manhattan. Homegrown cooks learned the lessons of the day and presented sophisticated diners from coast to coast with morels foraged in Michigan woods and hitherto neglected sea urchin gonads from Pacific waters. Aided by food processors, modish restaurants offered julienned vegetables of every hue with each floridly designed entrée. Following the lead of their French mentors, they were open to ideas from cooking traditions around the world, mixing all the great ethnic and national dishes in a mishmash of eclecticism that is every bit as intricate in its way as were the now-abandoned platters of yesteryear.

Even this superficial analysis of nouvelle cuisine would have surprised most of its happiest consumers, but there was more to this global movement in the kitchen than unfamiliar ingredients and painterly plates. Considered historically, nouvelle cuisine, as I argued almost thirty years ago, had deep roots in European gastrolinguistic tradition and was the logical conclusion of centuries of change in the way food was brought to the table and served to individual diners.

I thought about these matters first during a wedding in New Haven, in 1985, when I meditated briefly in a small church about deconstruction (then the latest fad in French literary analysis, which had captured the energies of the Yale English department) and its relation to trends in food. Almost all of the original claims made about and for the nouvelle cuisine had turned out to be exercises in public relations, but everyone who had experienced the food itself knew that it had a coherence, a recognizable cluster of characteristics. It was a style.

But it was a sly style, one whose true nature had barely ever been discussed by its practitioners. They were not shy, but the language they used was almost an ideal text for deconstruction because it was so purely metaphorical. I was using language here in a broad sense to include both chefs' words—their menu language and their recipes—as well as their dishes.

The world of nouvelle cuisine, I argued in *Natural History*, is a forest of symbols and allusions that the knowledgeable diner can "read" and decode, much as a literary deconstructionist might decode the figurative code of a poem. Classic cuisine was also a code, literally, couched in the language of menus and cookbooks. Dishes were identified with terms such as "Montmorency" and "Paloise," words that in ordinary speech refer to people and places but that in the world of traditional haute cuisine denoted, respectively, a roast duck sauced with cherries and a béarnaise sauce made with mint instead of tarragon. In most cases these chefs' terms were a pure code without even a tangential connection to their names' everyday referent. Espagnole sauce was in no way Spanish. The old culinary language simply gave names to dishes that honored people and places and rarely offered the uninitiated any direct information about the dish they were going to get.

The leaders of nouvelle cuisine were all trained in this nomenclatural code. They knew exactly what garnishes and sauce went with *sole à la normande*. The sole, poached in fish and mushroom stock, was surrounded by poached mussels and shrimp with a line of four poached oysters and four fluted mushroom caps alternating down its center. All of this was coated with *sauce normande*, an elaborate concoction of fish stock, mushroom and mussel cooking liquids, egg yolks and cream, and then additionally garnished with six truffle slices and six croutons cut in lozenges alternating around the perimeter of the sole. Four gudgeons, the freshwater fish *Gobio gobio*, fried at the last minute and themselves decorated with paper sleeves, were arranged on the platter with four medium crayfish. All the elements were compulsory; not until 1912 did Escoffier finally concede, in parentheses, that the truffles were optional.

The names of traditional haute cuisine dishes were, although sonorous, primarily useful as shorthand devices. They performed a real service for waiters, who did not have to memorize and then rattle off the four canonical garnishes associated with *rôti de veau Maubeuge*. Haute cuisine lingo saved everyone the bother we now endure from waiters who do not benefit from a convenient code and have to tell you that tonight's special is moose haunch with wild rice balls, broiled shiitake mushrooms and a partridge in a pear mousse. Wouldn't it be easier if that particular collection of foods were always identified as moose Mamaroneck?

Yes, it would be simple, but the culinary world we live in is an unsettled place. You can almost count on not getting moose with the same accompanying side dishes on another night in another restaurant (or often not even in the same restaurant).

But in the world set down in Escoffier's *Guide culinaire*, chefs did repeat the official garnish combinations. Over the 150 years that stretched from the time of Carême, in the early nineteenth century, until the dawn of nouvelle cuisine, French chefs refined a closed system of dishes whose basic unit was a serving platter dominated by a main food item—say, a roast—tricked out with its prescribed garnishes. Nouvelle cuisine not only abandoned the old culinary code and its heraldic certainties of *garniture* and presentation, it also abandoned platter service itself and substituted for it an equally intricate method of service based on individual plates arranged in the kitchen and then brought out to diners.

These attacks on the structure and meaning of the old style of dining are the truly revolutionary part of nouvelle cuisine, but the threat to the old order was masked in many ways. Nouvelle cuisine was marketed as the cuisine of modern slim people who valued fresh food or food presented with streamlined simplicity and provocative ingredients. All those elements were present and important, but they fronted for the real revolution, which transformed the old code by repurposing it as material for a most elaborate system of culinary parody, punning and metaphor.

Nouvelle cuisine looks at Escoffier through the wrong end of the telescope. It puts ironic quotation marks around Carême and sets the old code in italics so that the old words mean something else, are metaphors for new ideas for which no names previously existed.

In the dawn of the nouvelle era, gastronomic pilgrims trekked to dismal Roanne, near Lyon, to eat chez Troisgros, where they were served the great prix fixe menu of the postwar period: that deceptively dull-looking black-gray thrush pâté flavored with juniper berries, then thin slices of salmon in sorrel sauce, followed by local Charolais beef in an intense but transparently clear brown sauce and, finally, many, many desserts.

I ate this meal in 1969, the same year the term *la nouvelle cuisine* was coined by Gault and Millau to describe the food on the maiden flight of the supersonic jet passenger plane the Concorde.

The Troigros brothers' chaste dishes embodied the key elements of the mature movement. The salmon dish, especially, was a sign of things to come. The sauce was pulled together quickly, without flour for thickening, from a highly reduced fish stock, crème fraîche and sorrel. The taste was extraordinary, as was that of the salmon, almost Japanese in its near rawness. And what might be called the design of the dish emphasized lightness with its unnaturally thin pieces of fish.

These were the things that caught my eye in 1969 in that poky little dining room near the Roanne rail station. But the most important feature of the dish was the name on the menu. If the salmon had been cooked until it flaked and if the sauce had been thick and conventional, this dish would still have been a symbol of revolt because of its witty name: *escalopes de saumon*. The Troisgros brothers were serving salmon scaloppine. They had transferred (metaphorized) a classic (foreign) food idea onto a surprising and provocative new form. The sharp-eyed diner would notice that the chef had cut the salmon into thin flat slices, or scallops, and then had pounded them thinner, just as an Italian chef would have pounded veal scallops, except that the Italian would have pounded the veal because he wanted to make it tender as well as attractively thin. Pounding salmon will indeed change its texture in a minor way, but the main gain was conceptual. The thin salmon pieces were mock scaloppine. They were delicious, but they were also witty.

After the Yale wedding, I looked at my library of nouvelle cuisine cookbooks and menus with this in mind and found abundant examples of this metaphorical principle at work. Paging through *The Nouvelle Cuisine of Jean and Pierre Troisgros*, I noticed a vegetable terrine that was a playful nonmeat copy of a traditional meat terrine and a recipe for oysters with periwinkles—that is, shellfish topped with shellfish. Obviously not every nouvelle cuisine dish is a straightforward culinary pun or play on a figure of culinary speech, but almost invariably the memorable recipes start from a witty reinterpretation of a standard dish. It is this "literary" aspect that saves nouvelle cuisine from being merely a collection of outrageous novelties. The greatest failures of modern cooking have always been those entirely new dishes, concocted with no reference to the past. Its greatest triumphs have sprung from tradition seen through a glass brightly.

The other crucial feature of nouvelle cuisine—its studied and original arrangements of food on individual plates—is also a clever reaction to French tradition in the kitchen and at the dining table. The haute cuisine of my grandparents' time* called for

---

* They never ate or heard about such fancy food, of course, but even their shtetl-Yiddish culinary vocabulary could reflect Escoffier's jargon from time to time. My grandmother's chopped-meat *kutlett* was a country cousin of *côtelettes de veau Pojarski*. Both of these

edible designs to be executed on serving platters, which were then dismantled onto individual plates without much attention to "design." The original logic of the dish on the serving platter had been lost. This method of getting food to the table was called Russian service. Whether truly Russian or not, it emerged as a radical dining reform in the nineteenth century, quickly triumphed and held sway in luxury establishments right into the 1970s.

Russian service depended very heavily on the labor of waiters. In establishments that practiced this method to its fullest, meals were served on a platter, banquet-style, even if the diner was eating alone and had ordered something that could just as easily have been put intact on a plate in the kitchen and brought right to the table. Instead, *sole meunière* would be presented in a serving dish, finished with the canonical sizzle on a tableside hot plate (*réchaud*), then transferred to the plate at a buffet or rolling table near the dining table.

Anyone over the age of fifty will have no trouble recalling such meals. Russian service may have reached its perigee with dishes that were flamed tableside. Waiters turned into Prometheus, bringing fire to cognac and ladling the resulting vaporous blue-haloed liquid over steaks and, most dramatically, crêpes Suzette.*

It took most of the rest of the century for Russian service to sweep away its predecessor, French service. Gone, finally, were the simultaneous profusion of dishes, the architectural table deco-

---

patties were invigorated with chopped onion. Both emanated from the Russian empire. Pojarski, by legend, improvised the first of his eponymous patties for Czar Alexander I (who ruled from 1777 until 1825) out of veal, because he didn't have any beef for the chops the autocrat was demanding. Evidently, Pojarski didn't have veal chops either, but he ground up the meat he did have, perhaps veal shoulder, and then formed the chopped meat into the shape of a chop (*côtelette* or, literally, riblet). Grandma Mary knew nothing about any of this, had never heard of Pojarski and made no effort to shape her oniony beef *kutletts* (stressed on the last syllable) into chops.

* After Suzanne Reichenberg (1853–1924), a French actress whose stage name was Suzette. In 1897, she played a crêpe-making maid at the Comédie Française.

ration and the sculptural set pieces (*pièces montées*) that had marked the grandiose age of Carême. Russian service, championed in the 1860s by the influential chef Félix Urbain Dubois, allowed people to eat one dish per course. As a result, chefs turned to perfecting each individual dish instead of concentrating on an array of dishes. This led to platters bristling with ancillary garnishes. But in less than a century, dissatisfaction with these baroque arrays led to a further reduction in the scale of food presentation. Nouvelle cuisine restricted itself to the individual plate.

This reduction of the field of display—from table (medieval/French service) to platter (Russian service: later nineteenth century to 1965) to plate (1965 through the present)—followed along with a historical change in dining habits, from the self-service smorgasbord-like public dining of the late medieval and early modern eras to a waiter-finished, à la carte–style restaurant world to the kitchen-plated style of contemporary, post-nouvelle dining.

This evolution of presentation corresponded to an overall shift in restaurant staffing, from the servitors of French service—the waiters who cooked tableside, who had evolved from the footmen who set out the food and carved the meat for the medieval table—to the servers with cooking skills of Russian service to the nouvelle cuisine's noncooking, unskilled plate distributors.

Fluctuations in the cost of labor and the levels of skill available in those three periods played an important role in determining how food was brought to diners. Very cheap labor in the late medieval and early modern era made it possible to staff noble and nouveau riche dining rooms with hordes of footmen, most of them unskilled except perhaps at carving large pieces of meat. In the post-1900 world of rising literacy within the urban working class, overall wages rose, but semiskilled waiters could take pressure off the kitchen staff and do double duty as food deliverers. After World War II, the cost of labor rose again. Chefs streamlined their kitchen procedures, via the less laborious style of the "lighter" dishes of nouvelle cuisine, and eliminated the need for waiters with culinary skills by handing off completely plated individual dishes to unskilled waiters in the kitchen.

By the 1980s, this historic shift was complete. Diners had blithely accepted the new style, as if pictorial plating of slimmed-down, ironically deconstructed variations on traditional recipes was the normal thing to expect in serious, up-to-date restaurants. So was the increasingly exotic and cosmopolitan sourcing of ingredients, methods and recipes. But the diet-food tag persisted, and the chastely plated dishes featured in nouvelle cuisine–inspired restaurants left many diners who were accustomed to larger portions feeling as if they'd been subjected to a prettified form of a weight-loss regimen.

The emblematic American restaurant of that moment, Chez Panisse, was transforming itself from an outpost of simple French cooking in northern California into the sanctuary of locavore vegetable purity it continues to be today.

Chez, as its Berkeley habitués call it, was anything but a healthy, up-from-the-soil, hyper-Californian shrine in its formative era. The mother of it all, Alice Waters, evolved out of the political radicalism on the Berkeley campus into a food activist during a study year in France in 1964. A dinner in Brittany converted her forever to the simple beauties of French food. "I've remembered this dinner a thousand times," she told John Whiting in 2002.* "The chef, a woman, announced the menu, cured ham and melon, trout with almonds, and raspberry tart. The trout had just come from the stream and the raspberries from the garden. It was the immediacy that made those dishes so special."

Back in Berkeley, Waters began seriously cooking French food

* http://www.whitings-writings.com/essays/chez_panisse.htm

at home. In 1971, with financial backing from friends, she took over a Craftsman-style house and began serving family-style meals to the public. The name of the place also reflected her passion for French provincial culture. Panisse is a character in the trilogy of 1930s films based on plays by Marcel Pagnol about lower-class life in the port of Marseilles. Panisse is also the name of the chickpea-dough fritters typical of the Mediterranean coast of France from Marseilles to Nice.

So the roots of Waters's new restaurant were blatantly French, but her particular connection with French cuisine involved a vivid, if romanticized, vision of its connection to extremely local food sources. One may reasonably wonder if those primordial trout had actually been hooked on a fly the morning before she ate one. The norm, at any rate, even for very meticulous, family-run restaurants, would have been a tank or a pond supplied by a commercial *fournisseur*.

This is not to malign the freshness of the trout, only to cast doubt on the accuracy of Waters's tourist-eye romanticism. Paul Bocuse exploited a similar credulity in journalists like me. We usually did not stop to ask ourselves how it was that sea bass had turned up in the fresh waters of Lyon's twin rivers, the Rhône and the Saône.

At any rate, there can be no doubt that Waters impelled her new restaurant in a direction known much later as locavore. If her dwarf vegetables actually came from a farm near San Diego, hundreds of miles away, they were still native Californian. Her berries were foraged not far from Berkeley, by a tetchy fellow who wrote me a menacing letter when I quoted Alice describing the scratches he endured in order to bring her wild berries.

And as the daily set menus at Chez Panisse turned increasingly eclectic under a regularly changing cast of chefs, the emphasis on local, hands-on, nontoxic ingredients became the restaurant's central enduring theme. Chez Panisse began as a clever pastiche of meridional French home cooking that branched out into other kinds of simple food. It was and is a form of *auberge*, an inn with a table d'hôte. Hooray for all that, but even forty years ago, when a diverse nouvelle American cuisine was emerging all over the country, Chez Panisse wasn't serving it.

To do that, you had to know what traditional American cooking had been. You had to be interested in making modern versions of authentic survivals of regional cooking that had first evolved in pioneer days, during those creative moments of scarcity when settlers arrived in unfamiliar wilderness and were forced to produce hybrid meals, using the unfamiliar foods they found to make improvised versions of the recipes they had brought in their heads. In the Southeast, for example, slaves adapted the West African technique of deep-frying flour-coated foods to local ingredients and invented southern fried chicken and hush puppies. Because cornmeal was abundant, they substituted it for the native African black-eyed-pea flour they knew from home. Food historians of transatlantic black foodways, including Jessica Harris, documented this process. In the later 1970s, I began to hunt for authentic, specific regional dishes produced by the collision of immigrant pioneers with American conditions of pioneer days—a colonial form of unconscious nouvellization.

Adjustments frontier cooks made to foods they knew from their home countries in order to adapt them to culinary possibilities in a newfound land generated the diverse set of regional specialties that flourished all over America before the homogenizing effects of interstate highways and a system of increasingly anonymous food supply pushed these local cuisines into darkness and disuse. Yes, there were bodacious survivals, especially in economic backwaters like Cajun Louisiana and hispanophone New Mexico. But even in these places, much of what the casual visitor could run up against was adulterated and for show, at fairs and other commercialized focuses of regional self-celebration and hokum.

Over the course of time, I would write about these and other matters for *Natural History*. But when I was hired in 1974 by Alan Ternes, all he told me was that my column should "reflect the various fields in which the Museum of Natural History intersected with what people ate." And he wanted me to attach a germane recipe to each column.

I'd started out thinking that for a magazine celebrated as the vehicle for Margaret Mead's anthropology, I should try to consider cuisine as a facet of ethnography. This turned out to be a wide-open field, since anthropologists had by and large ignored what the people they studied ate. Even anthropologists who specialized in material culture had concerned themselves with tools and boats, or with tattoos and metalwork, but they'd largely left the business of writing down recipes from authentic ethnic cooks to nonacademic cookbook authors, and there were few enough of them venturing into the unplumbed outback of the vanishing preliterate world.

There was one shining exception to this, the very eminent French cultural anthropologist Claude Lévi-Strauss. His deep analysis of the mythology of the Bororo culture of central Brazil centered on the symbolism of the edible. Lévi-Strauss's monumental *Mythologiques* ranged much further than that, but its first volume, *The Raw and the Cooked*, had appeared in English not long before (1969), and the rest of the tetralogy was not completely anglicized until 1981.

Highly theoretical, yet dazzlingly gymnastic, this was a way of talking about food that I hoped to imitate in my column. Indeed, Lévi-Strauss had already influenced the treatment of primitive language and myth and culture in my novel *Native Intelligence* (1975), which reworked some of the traditional Amazonian stories Lévi-Strauss had found recorded in the *Enciclopédia Boróro*, a compendium compiled by Salesian missionaries to the Amazon and then deconstructed by Lévi-Strauss into a gastrocosmology.

So it was a natural step for me to infiltrate heavy doses of symbolic anthropology into my two-thousand-word essays on food in *Natural History*. This Lévi-Strauss Lite phase came to an abrupt halt when Ternes spiked my column on the meaning of blood in world cuisine, which included references to blood in the Eucharist as well as to the initiation ceremony of the Hell's Angels, in which the novitiate consumed the menstrual blood of his moll directly from the source, in front of the assembled Angels.

Alan did print my deliberately provocative column on cannibalism, but it strained his patience. I surveyed the entire ethnographic literature on cannibalism with the goal of determining which cuts were preferred on gustatory grounds.* For an illustration, I pointed the magazine's art department to the iconic image of cannibalism, an engraving purportedly based on an actual sighting by the artist of a missionary being cooked in a pot by savages somewhere in deepest Amazonia. And, for the obligatory recipe, I adapted the haute cuisine dish *pain de cervelle,* a sort of calf's-brain pudding or loaf, but with the ingredient line altered to read "1½ pounds brains of any higher mammal."

Carol Breslin, who handled my *Natural History* copy with intelligence and courtesy for twenty years (I must have seemed like a cream puff compared to her husband, Herbert, the hilariously undiplomatic manager of Luciano Pavarotti), revealed to me that, because I had stepped over the line this time into real anthropology, she'd felt compelled to procure a professional reading. The referee she chose loathed the column.

At the time, there was a fashionable theory going around that cannibalism was largely a xenophobic construct of European inter-

---

* Fingers took the palm.

lopers into exotic cultures and that where it had occurred, it was a reasonable response to desperate shortages of animal protein in the diet, not much different from the behavior of the modern cannibals who had eaten other passengers' flesh after their plane crashed in a remote part of the Andes. My reader, a proponent of this materialist, proto-Marxist explanation of tribal cannibalism, covered the margins of my galleys with testy dismissals of my "naive" repetitions of faulty anecdotes about pervasive ritual cannibalism and the chop-licking consumption of defeated neighbors, all drawn from academic journals. But he reached his highest point of dudgeon over the recipe. "I doubt," he thundered inaudibly, "that the author could distinguish the brain of a human from that of a large lizard."

Carol showed me these fulminations with high humor. The column appeared intact, although, mysteriously, many copies lacked the illustration. But then, at lunch, Ternes said, over coffee: "Why don't you drop the anthropology. It's not a real science. Try plants instead. That's what most food is, anyway."

Alan was always right.

I didn't know the first thing about botany. Nevertheless, edible plants, their origins, their lore, the incredible ingenuity with which cooks had exploited them—such questions kept me happily occupied over many years. My lack of training in the field was never a real hindrance. The nontechnical material was so rich, and so easily available, that after locating reliable sources, I found it a simple matter to assemble compilations of information about the horticultural conquest of the world by edible flora: by Indian mangoes tended in pots on shipboard until they could be safely naturalized in the Americas or by the many and surprising uses of the invaluable New World cassava plant—toasted grits (*farofa*) in the Brazilian national dish *feijoada*, bread I saw made on open fires in the Caribbean, as well as tapioca Mom had served in pudding.

Every year, I made a summer trip to the Caribbean to investigate yet another exotic plant. *Natural History* sold travel ads to the islands for a fall issue, and I provided editorial matter to go with them, columns based on sweaty summer interviews with taro gardeners in Monserrat and a lady in Santo Domingo who concocted jelly from the pendulous fruit of the cashew (the more familiar nut, as I pointed out, is a dead ringer for the seed concealed in the pit of the mango, which, like the cashew, is a member of the Anacardiaceae family, as is poison ivy).

I saw these fruits during the summer of 1992, as the guest of the government of the Dominican Republic, a repressive pseudo-democracy run by Joaquín Balaguer, who had gained power as a puppet of the murderous dictator Rafael Trujillo. But I was very happy to cross paths with the amiable Henri Gault, he of the Gault-Millau guide, an avatar of Jean Gabin in his craggy looks and bluff manner.

I discovered evidence of recent Lebanese influence on Dominican foodways in a neighborhood near the hotel, where a sign in front of a house advertised *quipe,* a Hispanic version of kibbeh, the pounded raw lamb–bulgur delicacy of Lebanon.

I spent my last night in the Dominican Republic playing black-jack in the hotel's dark and deserted casino. Sitting next to me at the table, not gambling, was the California wine writer Robert Finigan, who distracted me from my losses with a story from his former career as a management consultant in Japan, where he had learned to speak the language fluently.

One night in midwinter, he found himself in Wakkanai, the northernmost city in Japan, which, with an annual snowfall that can reach 250 inches, is among the snowiest populated places on earth. Finigan trudged through the snow to dinner in a nearby restaurant, empty except for a table occupied by an elderly couple in traditional garb. From across the dining room, they appeared to be greatly enjoying their meal.

Finigan called over a waiter and said in Japanese, "I'll have exactly what they're having." Minutes later he was startled by loud shrieks. He looked up from the book he'd been reading and saw the Japanese couple fighting to keep the waiter from taking away their plates and bringing them to him.

By 1992 I had long since established myself as an essayist on edible plants in *Natural History*. I often received letters from real botanists all over the world, asking for reprints of my columns. Usually, they addressed me as Dr. Sokolov. I really was operating in a serious academic context, as a kind of functioning botanist, and I came to see that I had a specialty. I was what was called an economic botanist; I studied plants in human affairs. There was even a publication in "my" field, the *Journal of Economic Botany*.

One day, I found a complete run of it in the stacks of the library at the American Museum of Natural History, where my connection to the museum's magazine gave me a plenipotentiary ID card. I was an "outside contractor" and could enter the museum and all its most guarded places at any hour. I rarely went to that library, since the museum had ceded the acquisition of books on plants to the New York Botanical Garden in the Bronx. Yet I particularly loved to poke in when the public couldn't, strolling early in the morning through the Andean dioramas, alone with the pumas and guanacos, the recorded noises of their snuffling and amorous crashes against each other incessantly looped and relooped, an eerie mammalian aria da capo, da capo.

Sometimes I continued upstairs, where there was a Xerox machine I could use for free in the library stacks, which, for a time, had plastic sheeting over a whole section, to protect the books from a leak in the roof. The reference room was presided over by a fierce woman of Middle European background whose desk was covered with flowering plants I could not have identified if asked. When I admired them, she responded fiercely, with an unleavened accent, "They say I can make a pencil bloom."

Then, just as I was settling into my role as the Linnaeus of comestible roots and leaves, Alan uprooted me from the soft bed of economic botany and sent me on the road, like one of those potted mangoes, to hunt down American regional foods, old-fashioned dishes threatened with extinction, like the black-footed ferret. I would spend two years doing it.

We both assumed that corporate agriculture, Big Ag, and all the other soul-crushing juggernauts of modern American life were smothering the last vital signs of regional food. But in almost every case, we found a dynamic revival of foodways, a supposedly vanished dish or abandoned ingredient that ought to have died out from neglect.

I say "we" because I had a partner in those travels, Adelaide de Menil, a photographer who worked much harder than I did, lugging equipment and getting down in the dirt to capture the morels in Michigan and roughing it in the Colorado high desert north of Rifle to record a sheep drive.

When we started out, I thought the way to find endangered foods was to flip through sources like my former colleague Jean Hewitt's *The New York Times Heritage Cookbook* and then make a blizzard of phone calls to the region, to find practitioners of the vanishing dish and set up appointments with them. This turned out to be a waste of everybody's time. There were sources you could find that way, but precisely because you could connect with a Pennsylvania Dutch flannel-cake vendor from your desk in New York, it almost guaranteed that she was an inauthentic exploiter of a pioneer dish whose only nexus to its colorful past was cash.

We quickly learned that winging it was the surest way to find the folks we wanted to find. Most of them did not advertise in the

Yellow Pages or feel comfortable making appointments. Since a great many of them were either active farmers or close to the land, on arrival we would check in first with the local county agent. These emissaries of the federal Department of Agriculture know everything about their bailiwick. They know who grows what crops and, through their work with families in the still great 4-H program, they know who cooks seriously in the old way, or who continues to cultivate crops or grow fruit that's too old-fashioned and unsalable even to get mentioned in the Ag Department's statistical publications.

After a while, we would just fly in to a place known, or usually formerly known, for a regional food and drift around the landscape until we found someone eager to cook it for us or show us his carefully tended plants.

These were not media-savvy people, but once we found them, they invariably turned out to be great interviewees, because we were often the first people who'd ever asked them about a passion that filled them with joy—and gave them an outlet for a missionary zeal for keeping alive a message that had all but lost its original audience.

Helen Sekaquaptewa, the mother of the Hopi tribal chairman, queenly at the wheel of a brand-new pickup, took me to her ranch house in New Oraibi, Arizona, to show me how to make *pö-vö-pi-ki*, or blue marbles, an "easy" Hopi breakfast dish. She stirred together a straightforward dough of blue cornmeal and boiling water and rolled it into small blue orbs, which she then poached. Getting the texture right is a matter of exquisite knack, a *tour de main* she learned as a girl in a traditional household.

Part of that same training taught Mrs. Sekaquaptewa how to make piki, the apex of Hopi blue-corn cookery. She told me how, having returned from a missionary school in 1910, she learned to make a stone piki griddle, starting with a granite slab and polishing it smooth, by hand, with pebbles. She also ground blue corn into flour, working it between two stones, one held in the hand, until she produced a very fine blue flour, much finer than the meal for sale in a nearby grocery.

"We have electric mills now," she told me. "It was hard work in my time, with stones, but good exercise. No one had a big stomach."

But the Hopi ritual calendar had kept piki alive among the eight thousand ethnic Hopis—that and their isolation in the high mesas of northeastern Arizona. I saw this in action at the Niman dance. Kachina dancers at Shungopavi, on Second Mesa, moved slowly with the precision of Rockettes, chanting, elaborately masked and feathered, sashed and buskined, consecrating the ground of the plaza with cornmeal, while an eagle chained to a nearby rooftop flapped its wings. When the kachina dancers disappeared into underground kivas, Hopi children passed out rolls of crisp blue paper-thin piki, translucent sheets of blue cornmeal that had started out as a film of dough on a stone griddle.

For me, piki was the most unadulterated example of all threatened American regional foods, enmeshed in the same civilization that had invented it centuries before Columbus. That culture had survived under constant threat, first from the Hopis' Navajo neighbors, then from white settlers, and, by the time I came to their mesa villages, from electric flour mills and supermarket blue cornmeal. But piki, because of the difficulty of making it, would never be the centerpiece of a Hopi-themed fast-food chain.

You might think that other First American foods would be just as difficult to assimilate into the American way of life, but the recent history of Navajo fry bread teaches a different lesson, as I learned in Salt Lake City. I hadn't intended to investigate Navajo food in the capital of Mormonism. Indeed, I went to some trouble to get invited to lunch at the official cafeteria in the headquarters of the Church of Latter-day Saints in the Lion House, once the home of the early Mormon leader Brigham Young.

In *Lion House Recipes,* the cookbook I acquired there, I found almost no purely local dishes, just an unreconstructed expression of mainstream middle-American food: Jell-O salad, pies, meats and potatoes. The sole exception was the anomalous Utah scone, a deep-fried bread fashioned from a sweet yeast dough cut in two-inch squares. They were nothing like the muffiny scones of Britain, which are usually baked and never deep-fried.

It was not hard to sample homegrown scones in Salt Lake City. Usually served with butter and honey, they popped up on breakfast menus and at a fast-food chain called Sconecutter. But where did they come from? They had clearly not arrived with the Mormon emigration. No, these New World scones reminded me of puffy deep-fried Navajo fry bread and even more of New Mexican sopaipillas, which are similar to fry bread but are also usually served with honey, like the Utah scones.

Lacking any hard evidence for their origin, I speculated in *Natural History* that the archetype for all these fried breads was a sopaipilla documented by Diana Kennedy, the English-born authority on Mexican food, in the Mexican state of Chihuahua, which shares a border with New Mexico. This primordial sopaipilla lacked yeast, a sign of its earliness. Mormon women, I argued, likely adopted this bread and assimilated it to their baking style with yeast and other raising agents, sugar and eggs, and further appropriated it with an English name.

I backed into yet another Anglo variation on First American food traditions at a convention of wild-rice growers in Grand Rapids, Minnesota. Wild rice, which is not a rice but a native grass that springs up in northern lakes, used to be very expensive because it had to be hand-harvested in the immemorial method devised by

Ojibwas, who would bend it over a canoe with a paddle and whack it until the seeds fell into the hull.

That picturesque harvesting method was about to disappear almost completely. Horticulturists had finally succeeded in hybridizing a nonshattering variety of wild rice that could be grown in paddies and harvested by combines, just like real rice and other grains. As excited lecturers pointed out at the Grand Rapids conference, wild rice had until then been left genetically unaltered by human ingenuity. Its seeds, maturing at different rates, would then fall off the seed heads into the lakes where the plants were growing, and therefore couldn't be harvested all at once. The Ojibwa method accommodated this naturally erratic biology: paddlers knocked down the mature seeds, which were about to fall of their own biological momentum into the lake. The unripe seeds clung to their grass tops and continued maturing. Paddlers had to keep returning for them until they had whacked down the whole crop.

The jubilant horticulturists at Grand Rapids had searched and found strains of wild rice that didn't shatter, didn't drop their seeds whenever they separately ripened. The nonshattering seeds clung to the plant so that they could all be harvested in one sweep. This made it possible to collect them like wheat or sorghum seeds.

Prescientific grain farmers had gone through a similar process of selection with rice and wheat and all the other grains in the dawn of human life, making way for an efficient harvest, the single most basic requirement of agriculture and for the settled form of life we call civilization. Now modern science had performed the same miracle with wild rice.

Not long after that meeting, commercial wild-rice paddies were established in California. The retail price of *Zizania aquatica* plummeted. Wild rice's future as a normal grain was secure, and only hobbyists and Ojibwa traditionalists continued to gather it in canoes.

By that point in my travels as an inquiring gastroethnographer, I had begun to assume that there would always be surviving examples of a regional food in its historic home, but that I would always be surprised by those foods when I actually saw them in situ. The facts on the ground were almost never what you'd expected as you'd boarded the plane.

In the Upper Peninsula of Michigan, the seemingly simple pasty, a meat pie brought there originally by Cornish settlers, was a focus of melting-pot controversy. The descendants of miners from Cornwall argued among themselves about whether an authentic pasty had to contain rutabaga, or if the chopped meat was un-Cornish without pork, or how fine to chop that meat. Some folks pulled the crust up from both sides and crimped it together at the top; others pulled it over from one side. These were good-natured arguments among kin. But a preponderance of pasty-proud Cornish-Americans around the pasty mecca of Marquette did not take kindly to late-coming Finnish immigrants and their descendants, who had adopted the pasty as their own in the Upper Peninsula and "mongrelized" it, or so it was said, with features of meat pies they remembered from Finland.

Hunting down the Key lime in south Florida, we drove from Miami to Key West, through a fog of disinformation propagated by hucksters for the indigenous Key lime pie. Very few producing trees of this small, spherical, green-skinned citrus fruit had survived the hurricane of 1926, none of them in commercial groves. And the groves had never been replanted.

So unless you knew someone with a backyard tree, the Key lime pie you were eating in Islamorada or Key Largo or anywhere else in this country, we established, had been made with the juice of the Tahiti or Bearss lime, the lemonlike citrus hybrid (sold green to make it easy for shoppers to distinguish it from true lemons) that is the lime of commerce in the United States.

When you squeeze a lime for a lime rickey or cut a section of a lime for a gin and tonic, it is a Tahiti lime—and, in the terms used by botanists and ordinary people outside this country, it is not a lime at all. The lime we call Key is the lime everyone else on the planet calls a lime, and it is also tastier and limier than the Tahiti.

Key lime pies containing Tahiti juice are, as I demonstrated in a side-by-side bake-off with a genuine Key lime pie, far less deliciously tangy than the real thing. And that real thing, the all-but-vanished Key lime, was in fact, further research showed, not in the remotest danger of disappearing from the planet. Indeed, it was flourishing from Mexico to Asia. Truth to tell, in most places not corrupted by marketing of faux Key lime pies and juice or of Tahiti limes, *C. aurantifolia* is the only known lime.

Such botanically wrong mislabeling is not exactly criminal, but it is as rife as shoplifting, and I did my best in *Natural History* to correct the misnomers that filled supermarket aisles.

Don't get me started about the yam, a large African root vegetable with white flesh, completely unrelated to and unlike the sweet potato, a usually yellow-fleshed Andean native often served on Thanksgiving tables as candied yams.

Similar confusion has helped keep Americans from enjoying one of the great native fruits, the small delectable persimmon that grows on big, hardwood trees of the ebony family from Florida and Texas to Central Park. But a blitzkrieg of marketing has filled market shelves with big sloppy Japanese *kaki* persimmons, while our superior American persimmons fall to the ground unattended and go smash.

I went to Brown County in southern Indiana, hard by the hamlet of Gnaw Bone, having been alerted to the presence thereabouts of *Diospyros virginiana* by those fellow stalkers of regional American specialties, Jane and Michael Stern. I roamed until I found the orange fruitlets, some already fallen, others pluckable from low branches, in an abandoned field—abandoned, that is, except by a feral dog, who bit me for intruding on his turf. I even was able to buy the misnamed, brownie-like persimmon pudding, for which Gnaw Bone is modestly renowned.

The renown would be much greater if misinformation—really plain old bad science masquerading as folk wisdom—had not kept this fine fruit from finding a market. It is simply not true that the native persimmon remains unacceptably astringent until the first frost, by which time many of the fruits have fallen from the tree, bruised themselves, rotted or been eaten by quadrupedal scavengers or frugivorous birds. Biology has also been, for the fruit of *D. virginiana*, a hampering destiny. The little orange orbs are overly endowed with seeds. The galumphing, often seedless *kaki* is much easier to eat.

Misnomer and its evil cousin fraud have also undercut the careers of two celebrated hunters' ragouts, Brunswick stew and burgoo. I was able to run down a 1907 recipe for Brunswick stew that allegedly preserved a dish invented by a black servant, Jimmy Matthews, on a hunting expedition into the woods of Brunswick County, Virginia, in 1828. Matthews served his white masters a squirrel stew. The heirloom recipe is clear on this point.

But you will basically never get squirrel in Brunswick stew today unless you shoot the squirrels yourself. The same is true of burgoo, an Ohio River valley specialty, whose name, derived from "bulgur," was originally applied to porridge by sailors who had encountered bulgur on shore leave in the Levant. In Kentucky and southern Indiana and Illinois on the other bank of the Ohio, burgoo once contained squirrel, but hasn't for many decades.

I tasted the peppery meat (chicken and beef) soup in the plain-faced river town of Owensboro, Kentucky, where serendipity led

me to Hardman's, a very unpretentious restaurant at which burgoo is a sideline. At Hardman's, as at fifteen other places in a city
then claiming fifty thousand inhabitants, mutton barbecue was the
draw. Two dressed ewes hung in a cold storage locker in back. The
ewes were stand-ins for the bison that had led the menu at Catholic
parish barbecues in the region in the nineteenth century. When
they ran out, the organizers of Owensboro fund-raising barbecues
substituted old ewes, whose flesh is thought to stand up as nicely to
open flame as the flesh of American buffalo.

The only other time I'd eaten mutton was as a *Times* reporter
in the cell block at the Brooklyn House of Detention. The slow-
cooked, smoky mutton in Owensboro was a huge improvement,
although the little restaurant was really a dump, with piles of old
newspapers filling a couple of the ten or twelve seats. The dead
ewes in the cooler added an eldritch touch, as did a third ovine
sizzling away in an open fire, which the place's sole employee kept
under control with a garden hose. A defunct Philco twelve-inch
television from the Eisenhower era watched over the scene like an
evil eye, lacking only a test pattern or an episode of *Kukla, Fran
and Ollie* or *Captain Video* to complete the time warp.

Seedy mise-en-scènes were often a backdrop to research into
regional American foods. What was the nadir of these expeditions
to the hinterland?

It was the coat closet (officially the evidence locker) in the
grim stone jail in Franklin County, Virginia, where I tasted seized
moonshine from repurposed plastic soda bottles at the invitation
of Sheriff W. Q. Overton. Franklin was said to be the leading bastion, and one of the last, of untaxed hooch distillation in America.

On the basis of this *dégustation*, I opined that moonshine was
a first cousin of grappa, then beginning its rise to chic, with the
same distinctive sour flavor, the result of a similarly thrifty, rustic style of production. Unlike manufacturers of politer forms of

distilled spirits, grappa makers and moonshiners did not throw out the initial spurt from the still ("the first puke," in Appalachian argot). This contains aldehydes, chemical components of alcohol that give both drinks, as well as their French (marc) and Spanish (*orujo*) cousins, their defining taste ("sourheads").

But moonshine got no respect, while grappa and marc graced fancy menus in Europe and increasingly in the United States.* I lamented this state of affairs and called for a national movement to encourage the legal manufacture and sale of moonshine. I also, unwisely, quoted a local newspaper editor who'd accused the publisher of a rival paper of fronting for the moonshine interests. Perhaps under the influence of the homemade booze in the jailhouse, I'd neglected to give the accused publisher a chance to defend himself. He, a former U.S. attorney in Virginia, sued me and *Natural History* for libel. The magazine, which carried no libel insurance, settled the case by paying a modest sum to the ex-prosecutor and persuading me (with the threat of leaving me to defend myself in a Virginia court) to sign a humiliating and false retraction published in *Natural History*.

I may have reached an even lower point as *Natural History*'s plant sleuth at the sloshed, sunbaked chili cook-off in the Texas ghost town of Terlingua, near a desolate stretch of the Rio Grande, where Texas Rangers waited for the drunk, self-appointed saviors of the U.S.-Mexican border's signature dish to weave into the night and fail a Breathalyzer test.†

A tall Humpty Dumpty kept flashing his Vietnamese driver's license to catch my attention long enough to try to sell me a box

---

* *Orujo* never made much of a splash outside Spain, but it is well worth asking for in Spanish restaurants.

† This was developed by an Indiana policeman named Robert Borkenstein, later a professor at Indiana University. The Breathalyzer was preceded by Rolla Harger's invention of the Drunkometer in 1931.

of his own commercial chili mix. And then there was the young man in a T-shirt that promoted a regional dish that had hopped the river from Mexico. The illustration made no sense until you read the caption under it on the shirt: "If God didn't want Man to eat pussies, why did he make them look so much like tacos?" While noncooking young women competed in a wet T-shirt contest and some young men took their pants off for a hairy leg competition, other very serious chiliheads stirred their pots. I watched the chili cooks closely and ended up admiring their dogmatic efforts to preserve the purity of a popular but often misunderstood regional dish. Texas chili, by the rules of the cook-off and according to the universal belief of Texas chiliastes, may contain no vegetable other than the onion. This exclusionary principle focuses the dish on its essential ingredient—beef—and segregates it from other regional chilis, such as New Mexico's, which contain beans.

So the wild, red-faced revelers at Terlingua, like the downmarket mutton-barbecuing Catholics in Kentucky and the Dogpatch, Virginia, moonshiners, were doing their part to uphold honorable food traditions, even if it meant risking trouble with the law in locations you wouldn't want your daughter to visit. I quite enjoyed the seediness and kept out of trouble with the law, although I was anxious about that libel retraction in *Natural History*, since it appeared soon after I had been hired to create a daily Leisure and Arts page for the *Wall Street Journal*.

Apparently, none of my new colleagues at the *Journal* read *Natural History*, or cared about the retraction if they did notice it. For the next nineteen years (1983–2002), I ran an eclectic page with articles that ranged over pretty much anything that wasn't economic or political news.

For twelve of those years, until I retired from *Natural History* in 1994, I continued to write that magazine's food column. At the

Journal, I made it a practice not to write about food, thinking that it was wiser to keep my arts journalism as separate as possible from my lingering career in food. I was concerned about diluting my authority as a cultural editor with a confusing presence in the paper as a food writer.

This policy, it seems, was not important to anyone but me. My boss, Robert L. Bartley, the neoconservative editor of the *Journal,* who ran the paper's three opinion pages (the editorial page, the op-ed page, and my page), never complained about my outside food column or the cookbooks I wrote while working for him. In fact, I think it increased my value in his eyes that I had a separate identity outside his world.

The *Natural History* column got written on weekends, and it continued to evolve in new directions through the 1980s and early 1990s, until I decided I'd done whatever I had it in me to do with it. I wouldn't have been able to put a succinct label on what I'd been doing, until the summer of 1981. That July, I flew to England to participate in the first public meeting of the Oxford Symposium on Food and Cookery, a weekend conclave of food historians, journalists, cooks and foodies from Britain and the rest of the world. I didn't know it then, but I would continue going to the Symposium almost every year thereafter, presenting papers, making friends and shaping this new intellectual force in the world of food as it shaped me.

In Oxford, for the first time, I found colleagues with a passion for studying food—and I found myself.

The Symposium had started out as a series of seminars on the "impact of science on the kitchen" at St. Antony's College, a relative upstart in Oxford founded in 1950 up the Woodstock Road from the medieval center of the university. The Symposium's original subject derived from the research of a highly unusual fellow, in both senses of the word. Alan Davidson, a retired British diplomat who had invented the field of gastroichthyology with practical guides to the seafood of the Mediterranean and Asia (including *Laotian Fish and Fish Cookery*), was the Alistair Horne Fellow at St. Antony's for the academic year 1978–79.

Davidson's sponsor in this unorthodox intrusion upon the college's normal diet of graduate research in the social sciences and international relations was Theodore Zeldin, a social historian of France. Davidson was not only intellectually eccentric in his focus on food but eccentric in the normal way, given to turquoise vintage sports jackets, an antique Bentley, Laotian string bracelets and the American screwball comedies of his youth, with which he was utterly besotted.

From their start in May 1979, the seminars attracted a diverse group of "students," from the physicist Nicholas Kurti to Britain's leading food writer, the literate and opinionated ("I hate people who eat duck at lunch") Elizabeth David.

Although the first series of symposia stuck to their technical subject—investigating the work of eminent food scientists of the past; Count Rumford, the inventor of the modern oven; and Justus von Liebig, the father of the bouillon cube—these were not conventional academic sessions. Word spread quickly. People who had theretofore pursued their interest in food history on their own now found a meeting place and flocked to it: restaurateurs, cooking teachers, food-oriented antiquarian booksellers, gastronomes— among them American expats and Dutch intellectuals.

The unexpected demand for places, and for continuing the program beyond Davidson's fellowship year, persuaded Zeldin and Davidson to create an annual symposium at St. Antony's that could welcome a sizable crowd.

The first of these meetings took place in 1981. Roughly 150 people attended, among them J. J. Flandrin, the doyen of French food historians; Rudolf Grewe, the editor of the first European cookbook, the fourteenth-century Catalan treatise *I Sent Sovi;* the food editor of the *London Observer,* Paul Levy; the Arabist and *Rolling Stone* writer Charles Perry; two American cookbook authors who had married rich and titled Englishmen;* a cookbook dealer; a cookbook shoplifter; experts on the cuisines of Sumatra, the Balkans, precolonial New Zealand; a colorful assortment of serious foodies;† and me.

I had persuaded Alan Ternes that I should cover the first international conference ever held in my "field." He agreed and kept sending me right through the end of my column, fourteen years later. That first year, right away in the registration line, I knew I was among real colleagues for the first time. Up until then I had been working in a vacuum. Here was a room full of people who'd been doing the same thing in isolation from one another. Now we were a community, all in one place, chattering away. And the name for what we were chattering about came to be "food history."

The topic of that intellectual love feast was National and Regional Styles of Cooking. And the papers were appropriately all over the map. Several were in French, among them Marie-Claude Mahias's analysis of Jain meals in northern India. But the papers weren't, and never have been, the only purpose of the Symposium, which is not a conventional academic meeting.

In the Symposium's early years, there were no academic pro-

---

* Such unions inevitably remind me of the lead-in to the daytime U.S. radio soap opera *Our Gal Sunday,* which I listened to devotedly during many bedridden weeks with severe cases of all three traditional children's diseases: "Once again, we present *Our Gal Sunday,* the story of an orphan girl named Sunday from the little mining town of Silver Creek, Colorado, who in young womanhood married England's richest, most handsome lord, Lord Henry Brinthrope. The story that asks the question: Can this girl from the little mining town in the West find happiness as the wife of a wealthy and titled Englishman?" The answer, on air as in life, was: Not always. The theme song was "Red River Valley."

† The term "foodie," according to the *Oxford English Dictionary,* was coined by Gael Greene in *New York* magazine in 1980, but the Symposium's Paul Levy and his coauthor, Ann Barr (also present at St. Antony's in 1981 and later years), made it famous in *The Official Foodie Handbook* (1984).

grams in food history or food studies. The whole idea of food history was a renegade notion, even a laughable notion in the hidebound world of university history departments. The professional scholars in attendance at that first symposium had not made their careers with their articles on food (with the exception of a few mainstream historians who had published or edited texts that happened to touch on food). The majority of the symposiasts were amateurs, serious intellectuals but amateurs nonetheless. In those days, no symposiast expected to advance an academic career with a paper she had submitted to this fledgling organization.

The structure of the meeting was deliberately informal. Papers were not read in their entirety—not read, in fact, at all but briefly summarized by their authors, usually in a panel with authors of essays with related subjects.

Plenary sessions in 1981 were even less structured. Basically, we sat in the dining room of St. Antony's and tried out our ideas on one another. It reminded me of a freshman-year bull session, but these were adults who knew things. Maria Johnson knew everything about the intricacies of Balkan regional foods, as an emigrant fluent in all the many languages spoken in this literally Balkanized former Ottoman territory. Sarah Kelly, a San Franciscan transplanted to German-speaking Europe, had made an encyclopedic study of baking in Germany, Austria and Switzerland, and shared it with us, analytically.

In the background, Alan Davidson and Theodore Zeldin hovered benignly. Neither of them ever gave a paper or joined in the discussions much. They were conducting a social experiment as well as a mildly subversive scholarly meeting. The Symposium had a deliberately unhierarchical, Summerhillian, sixtyish air of freedom and classlessness. Davidson and Zeldin were just Alan and Theodore. The Saturday lunch was a potluck affair, for which local symposiasts brought food from home and shared it in the most cosmopolitan display of exotic dishes anyone has ever seen under one roof. This lasted for years, until U.K. regulations about food served in public places snuffed it out. At the end of each year's weekend, there was a plenary session in which suggestions from the floor for the next Symposium were discussed and put to a vote. And if Theodore did somehow manage to guide the ultimate choice of topic in a direction he favored, the process was still public and nominally democratic.

I liked this libertarian approach to the intellectual study of sensuality. It suited my situation as an intellectual operating outside academia. The Symposium, as deliberately uninstitutional as an institution could be, seemed almost tailor-made for me. It did not offer me a career path, as an academic department would have. It was more like a club, in which all the members shared my previously idiosyncratic passions and pursuits.

But it lasted for only one weekend, once a year. And during the next twenty years, I was only a part-timer in the food world. For those two decades, I worked for Dow Jones & Co. Before I joined its *Wall Street Journal,* in my first real job since I'd left the *Times* in 1973, I edited a dreadful Dow Jones magazine called *Book Digest.* It was a magazine I'd never even heard of, and my connection with it began, fittingly, with a phone call from a man I'd never heard of either.

Francis X. Dealy, Jr., a dramatically good-looking former ad salesman, ran the business side of *Book Digest,* which did its tacky best to copy the *Reader's Digest* formula in the world of books. Basically, it ran excerpts of best sellers. I'm not sure I quite understood this, even after "Bud" Dealy tried to explain it to me. But I needed a job. I made an impressive enough living for a freelance journalist and writer of books, but that wasn't saying much. And I had two children in an expensive private school in New York City. So I accepted Bud's invitation to interview for the top editor's job.

I was in the competition because Peter Kann, the anointed successor to Warren Phillips as the Dow Jones chairman, had known me at the *Harvard Crimson* in the early 1960s and was a fan of mine. Phillips and Kann were about to hire a woman from the staff of *Ms.* magazine, Ruth Sullivan, to run *Book Digest*. In a final interview, as Ruth told me years later, they asked her if she'd had any experience editing men. Why, yes, she replied, she had edited Ray Sokolov.

This was true. She had edited a short piece I'd written for *Ms.* on the French Jewish philosopher Simone Weil.

Kann perked up at the mention of my name. He told Bud Dealy to find me. Bud succeeded, and I was hired.

Life as an executive at a major media corporation was beautiful. My office, on a high floor of a classy building at Fifty-seventh Street and Fifth Avenue, overlooked Bergdorf's and offered an unobstructed view above Central Park all the way to the Metropolitan Museum. I had been able to handpick an intelligent and amenable staff. The work was incredibly simple.

Each month, I would scan the best-seller list and buy the rights to reprint a short excerpt from a mix of those and other current books. Technically, such rights are known as second serial rights. First serial rights give a magazine (a serial publication) the right to publish material from a book before it is published. The *New Yorker* buys first serial rights and pays plenty for them. Second serial rights allow a magazine to publish material from a book after it is published. This is not a lively marketplace, but we managed. The problem was to sell subscriptions to readers and to sell ads. Our readers tended to be women over fifty living in retirement communities, a highly undesirable demographic.

This was dispiriting, but the end came soon. By the beginning of the summer of 1982, Dow Jones had shut down the magazine and fired the entire staff, except me.

Peter Kann said to me cheerfully, "You've wrecked our magazine. Come downtown and see what you can do to our newspaper." There ensued a kind of nirvana.

After some initial weeks with the *Wall Street Journal* news department, during which I wrote front-page features on the kiwi and tofu,* I moved upstairs to the neoconservative editorial page, where I'd been an occasional contributor of book reviews for years. Bob Bartley needed somebody to create a daily arts page, and he picked me.

I foresaw, correctly, that it would be easy and fun to fill a single page of the *Journal* every day by soliciting three to four pieces, mostly from freelances. New York was teeming with talented, lively cultural writers. Good ones needed only light editing. The less good ones I could edit without strain. In fact, I found it positively rejuvenating to rewrite a swatch of lame copy. It took me back to my twenties at *Newsweek,* when I often was assigned to take a file from a bureau reporter and, as we used to say, run it through my typewriter.

So life was a dream and stayed that way for me for nineteen years. All that time I worked at the same job, for the same intelligent boss. I disagreed with his political and economic views, but I could easily ignore his loony passion for supply-side economics, and he just as easily—actually, more easily—paid no attention to my views on classical music.

Also, the job came with an expense account. Like every other editor in town, I needed to meet with writers, and that is how I managed to stay current with the New York restaurant scene dur-

---

* After the kiwi article appeared (the fruit is really the Chinese gooseberry, but because the first big crops came from New Zealand, it was branded after New Zealand's mascot, the flightless bird called *kiwi* in Maori), I learned from a reader's letter that "kiwi" was airline slang for a terminated flight attendant (wings clipped). And, as part of my research on tofu, I got a hilarious quotation from my friend Maddie Lee about tofu tempura: she called it "deep-fried nothing."

ing the 1980s and 1990s. It was much better than being a restaurant critic. I ate only at good places, and I didn't have to write reviews. For most of this period, I continued to think about food for my *Natural History* column, and I produced four cookbooks, while I watched the food trends of the 1970s explode into the glamour scene of star chefs and the TV food hysteria of today.

Five

With Reservations

Shortly before nine on the morning of September 11, 2001, I leashed my dog, Duncan, and took him out for a walk in Greenwich Village. As we emerged from our gate onto Barrow Street, I looked left and right to make sure we wouldn't collide with a runner or surprise another dog. The coast was clear, but to my left I noticed a crowd of people standing in the middle of Seventh Avenue, facing south, downtown, and staring up. I joined them.

The north tower of the World Trade Center, hooded in smoke, had, as we eventually learned, been gored by American Airlines Flight 11, which smacked into its north face just below the building's top at 8:46 a.m. The sky, as everyone remarked, was eerily clear and blue, but even so, the second crash, of United Airlines Flight 175, into the south face of the south tower, between floors seventy-seven and eighty-five at 590 miles per hour at 9:03, although witnessed by our crowd in the street and by millions on television in real time, came from the opposite side of the towers and was easily mistaken for the exploding fuselage of the first plane.

Duncan and I went home to watch the coverage of this awfulness on television. I was shocked like everyone else that morning, of course. But since I was physically unharmed and not acquainted with any of the actual victims of the attacks, it took several months before I understood that 9/11 had had a decisive, violent effect on me. It ended my perfect life at the *Wall Street Journal*.

The *Journal*'s offices had looked directly at the Twin Towers from across West Street. Every weekday morning, when I wasn't on vacation or traveling for work, I took the No. 1 subway to Cortlandt Street and walked through the Trade Center underground concourse to our offices in Battery Park City, the enormous office and apartment building complex erected on landfill salvaged from the excavation for the towers.

For me, the Trade Center was not just something I saw from my office. I had had a direct personal and professional interest in the original excavation for the towers and in their construction. The World Trade Center's architect, Minoru Yamasaki, had been based in Detroit when I was growing up there. At the end of high school, I took his daughter Carol to the movies. The Yamasakis lived in a very American suburban house not designed by the architect, but he had put his stamp on the place with a traditional Japanese sand garden in the front yard. It disconcerted me on the summer night I came to pick up Carol Yamasaki, as did her grandmother, in a kimono, who thanked me at the door for being "so kind" to Carol.

So I felt kindly toward the Yamasakis, in turn, but I had not been able to avoid feeling a chill whenever I passed the brutalist towers and the inhumanly empty and cheerless space around them.

While the World Trade Center was still a construction site, I had gotten an assignment from the *New York Times Magazine* to write a piece about the revolutionary food-service system planned for the Twin Towers by the legendary restaurant impresario Joseph

Baum. Because of construction delays, I nursed that assignment for two years, hovering around the site until I could eat in the ingenious coven of intimate eateries that flowed one into another on the concourse, as well as in other more formal restaurants on higher floors, an integrated food-service network that culminated, literally, in Windows on the World, 106 floors above what eventually became Ground Zero.

My first meal of many at Windows was a preopening staff lunch, at which I interviewed the chef, who served me, as a sign of especial respect, part of the liver of a deer he'd shot over the weekend. It was raw and purple. Six Windows employees, including Baum's acerb and brainy consultant Barbara Kafka, were watching me. I bolted the organ, still icy from the refrigerator, slice by slice, in a panic relieved only by the site of the spike of the Empire State Building's broadcast antenna piercing the ocean of clouds three miles uptown, which blanketed everything else in Manhattan except it and us in thick fleece.

Milton Glaser, the eminent graphic designer who had collaborated on Baum's complex project, had copied the sky around us on a brighter day for the ceiling of a restaurant on the seventy-eighth floor, where there was a barber I went to for the view over the Hudson from his chair.

I did not make it to lunch in the towers on February 26, 1993, the occasion of the first terrorist attack on the World Trade Center. As lunchtime drew near, in order to pass the time until guests from Santa Fe arrived, I was listening on earphones to a recording of the original version of Arnold Schoenberg's *Verklärte Nacht*, which was written for string sextet, when, at 12:18 p.m., a boom blasted through the music. My first thought was: This piece is not scored for tympani. Then I looked out the window at my right elbow: smoke was pouring out of a ventilation baffle in the street nine floors below. Islamist terrorists had exploded a 1,200-pound bomb in a Ryder rental van parked in the underground garage of the Trade Center. Six people were killed. Smoke filled the towers, and fifty thousand were evacuated.

My intrepid New Mexican friends had been moving upward on an escalator to a covered bridge spanning West Street when the explosion hit and knocked out power to the escalator. After pausing for only a moment, they walked up the stalled stairway and continued on to my office. We ate in a little place on the water in the World Financial Center. I've forgotten its name and menu, but not the TV monitors over the bar, which dropped their usual fare of stock market news for coverage of the disaster across the street. Survivors, their faces black from smoke, trickled in steadily. With each arrival, applause broke out and we, the unharmed, bought them drinks.

After 9/11, the *Journal* opened offices for its staff in temporary locations all over Manhattan. Our least fortunate colleagues were exiled to the company's sprawling and cheerless complex in South Brunswick, New Jersey. Our page moved with the neocon editorialists and the Weekend section to a loft space in the garment center. I would never return as a staffer to 200 Liberty Street after the building was decontaminated and rehabbed, many months later. My job was eliminated in a brutal budget cut that did not stem the accelerating decline of the *Journal*'s fortunes, until its sale to Rupert Murdoch in 2007.

Getting forcibly "retired" in May 2002 did not surprise me. Even before 9/11, I had foreseen the future. In the spring of 2001, virtually every journalist over sixty on the paper, the core of its institutional memory, took early retirement. Then came a redesign and a restructuring, which reduced the presence of the Leisure and Arts page ("my" page) in the *Journal* from five days to three. We did pick up space in Weekend, but it wasn't really *ours*, in name or spirit, and our location on other days had been shifted from a key spot in the A section to the new fourth section, Personal Journal, a catchall of personal finance advice and soft news.

My job had shrunk in scope almost by half. Either someone was going to figure it out and fire me or I'd be twiddling my thumbs at my desk. One way or the other, I was going to need something to fill the slack time. I signed a contract with Susan Friedland at HarperCollins for a compendium of 101 recipes every literate cook should know (I asserted), which appeared in 2003 as *The Cook's Canon*. I also arranged to re-up as a classics graduate student at Harvard in order to finish my long-abandoned PhD.

It wasn't as though I had been brooding guiltily about that unfinished dissertation ever since I had forsaken classics for the Paris bureau of *Newsweek* in 1965. But I had never been able to cut the cord completely. From time to time, I would reread a book of Homer or Vergil (Book IV of *The Aeneid* for the Vergil bimillennium in 1970), and I couldn't bring myself to toss out the notes for my thesis on rare Homeric vocabulary in Theocritus, hundreds of three-by-five cards in a hinged maple box.

Then one night in early 2001 I ran into John Van Sickle, a Harvard classicist who had fetched up at the City University of New York. He handed me an offprint of his latest article on Vergil. I read it and noticed that the footnotes were full of references to lively-sounding recent work on the sources for Vergil's Eclogues, short pastoral poems modeled after Greek poetry of third-century B.C. Alexandria.

I mentioned this to John and observed that my notes for a thesis on Theocritus, the leading poet of the proto-Vergilians in his article, had survived the years in my attic.

"Why not give them to me?" he asked.

If this had been a scene in a comic book, a lightbulb would have gone on over my head. I thought: If a distinguished senior scholar like him is interested in them, maybe I should consider using them myself.

I checked. Even after thirty-five years and a boomlet in Hellenistic studies, no one had stumbled onto my thesis idea. Way back then, I'd noticed how Theocritus worked stunningly unusual Homeric vocabulary into his Idylls, which were very un-Homeric short poems about lovesick shepherds or other highly unepic, unheroic material. Those rare Homeric words stuck out like drawn swords at a tryst in a sheepfold.

An ancient reader from Theocritus's circle of scholar-poets at the Alexandrian library could not have missed these Homeric nonce words. Hellenistic literati knew *The Iliad* and *The Odyssey* by heart. So when they saw a word Homer had used only once in a contemporary poem, they would have automatically connected it with its original location in Homer. Just as automatically, they would have compared the two contexts in their minds, the original and the Theocritean. The pinpoint verbal link would have spotlit the contrast between Homer's bloody heroic universe and the soft, love-besotted pleasant retreats of Theocritus's bucolic brave new world.

I called the Harvard classics department to find out if my graduate work from the sixties was still valid toward the PhD. The secretary had no idea and referred me to the university registrar, who showed no surprise at all to be discussing readmission with a man who'd dropped out thirty-seven years before. They sent me a green, single-page form. I sent it back. There were three other requirements.

First, I owed the richest learned institution in the world a $150 "reactivation fee" for every term for which I had not registered. This would have amounted to $11,100 for the seventy-four terms I'd been AWOL, but there was a cap of $1,000. That I could afford.

Second, I had to submit an official copy of my graduate school transcript bearing the seal of the university. To accomplish this, I sent a $3 check by snail mail to Harvard's archival division, which sent me back the transcript, also by snail mail. I then put the transcript in another envelope and mailed it back to Cambridge, to another university office a short walk from the place that had issued the transcript. So much for the information highway.

Finally, and most challenging, I needed a letter of recommendation from a member of the department. Every professor I had known was dead, except for one. Wendell V. Clausen, my original thesis advisor, was seventy-eight and, though retired from a very eminent career as a Latinist and student of Hellenistic poetry, he was also emeritus and therefore technically still a member of the department.

He wrote the letter. I was readmitted, earlier than I had expected. But I had to finish work on *The Cook's Canon* before I could start on the dissertation. So I spent a year researching 101 classic recipes I thought should be part of everyone's culinary background, before I dived into reading all the scholarship on Hellenistic poetry that had come out since my flight from antiquity in 1967.

Then I wrote the thesis,* without any of the career anxiety that had made me leap to the safety of *Newsweek* in 1965. And I got the doctorate in 2005—June 9, to be exact. I even attended commencement in the Harvard Yard and sat in the front section once again (the right side, reserved for PhD's, instead of the left, for undergraduates, where I had once shared the front row with the other AB summas), close enough to see porky Harvard president Larry Summers peer with half-shut beady eyes out on the thousands of students and their guests. Henry Louis Gates was up on

---

* "Herding Homer: Rare Epic Vocabulary and the Origins of Bucolic Poetry in Theocritus."

the dais, too. I'd seen him the week before at Columbia University, at the awards ceremony for the Pulitzer Prizes. "My" film critic at the *Journal,* Joe Morgenstern, had won the prize for criticism, the only Pulitzer "my" page had won in two decades. Nothing, apparently, became my career at the *Journal* so much as my leaving it.

You may be wondering why I didn't take my shiny new degree and find a job on some leafy campus teaching the young about the aorist optative or the joy of Sextus Empiricus.* Well, I really wasn't interested in teaching anywhere but Harvard, and Harvard wouldn't have me. I asked Richard Thomas, the head of the department, who had been on my dissertation committee, if I should apply for a job I'd learned about in an ad in the *Times Literary Supplement* of London. The minimum requirement was a dissertation in progress, and I already had the degree. Richard replied, "We're looking for someone for the long haul."

I was, by then, sixty-five years old, but far from senile, just too foolish not to have recorded this exchange, which would have given me a case to sue Harvard for age discrimination.

I did teach one semester at Columbia, which taught me once and for all that I had no aptitude or inclination for teaching. And, anyway, by then I was too busy traveling around the country trying out new restaurants for, yes, the *Wall Street Journal.*

Once again, I had been unexpectedly lured back into food journalism.

The enticing Mephistopheles who did the luring was Tom Weber. I remembered him as a young *Journal* reporter I'd met just after he'd gotten the go-ahead to do a piece on interactive porn websites, which meant he could tell models to do kinky things to themselves from the comfort of his *Journal* workstation. This would normally have been a firing offense, but Tom had obtained

---

* Respectively, a Greek tense and a Greek philosopher of the Roman Empire.

a license to ogle from his editor and he couldn't stop telling anyone who'd listen about his new assignment.

He'd advanced beyond that kind of thing by the time he called me. Tom was the editor in charge of the *Journal*'s new Saturday Pursuits section, a love child of the Friday Weekend section with a major commitment to covering food.

Would I like to try reviewing restaurants for Pursuits? I said I would. And that was that. For almost four years, during which time Tom lost his job to a much less talented careerist, I continued to be the *Journal*'s designated diner, until the Murdochniks finally got around to thinking they might as well put their stamp on food, now that they had brought the rest of the paper up to their antipodean standard of excellence.

Their decision to eliminate full-dress restaurant criticism from the paper made a kind of sense. Very few readers could actually dine in the places I'd been writing about, even though I'd scattered my visits around the nation. And I'd been spending plenty of money, almost $100,000 a year, on travel and restaurants. But I had apparently managed to swim beneath the notice of the managing editor, Robert Thomson. When I'd run the *Journal*'s arts page, I used to joke that it was a bit like being the medical editor of the *Christian Science Monitor*. I had been able to enjoy something like the same freedom of ignominy as Thomson's restaurant guy. The one time we met, at the insistence of one of his secretaries, he couldn't seem to think of anything to say to me.

His apparently complete indifference probably kept him from noticing what a well-kept, globe-trotting servitor I was, and delayed his drawing the conclusion that someone jetting off to Vegas, Reykjavik and London in the same month, and earning the paper's top freelance fee every other week, was someone whose work might be worth serious scrutiny. Eventually he figured it out, or somebody else told him my gravy train wasn't the right vehicle for food in the weekend *Journal*, which he was revamping in the image of London's Saturday *Financial Times*.

Even the best, most sympathetic editorial supervision isn't often much better, from the writer or reporter's point of view, than having a KGB minder with strong ideas about how his agents should do their jobs. But until Thomson's predecessor had sent Tom Weber packing, I'd been reporting to a smart journalist who had a great many acute things to say about how my coverage of American dining should be shaped.

Weber pressed me into doing cover pieces for the section on the country's best hot dog joints, its best burgers and its best barbecue. Weber also had inherited the old *Journal*'s passion for the "nut graf," a paragraph high up in the story that summed up the point of the exercise and justified it. To me, this was a clunky interruption of the actual story, and I did my best never to force one into my columns, which meant that the editor I reported to directly had to make me write one or put one in herself. But I came to miss these bearable and sometimes genuinely helpful interferences after Weber left and was replaced with a regime that virtually never paid any attention to what I was doing, unless a reader made them think I'd committed an error worth correcting. After Weber, I never wrote a cover story, not even the projected takeout on America's greatest pizzas, a plan that was swept aside after the Thomson regime decided to lead the section each Saturday with a topical essay of great length and deathless wisdom penned by a writer of renown.

In truth, I had begun to enjoy my pop-food odysseys. Going to Decatur, Alabama, to check out Big Bob Gibson's barbecue was not that different from the trips I'd once taken so proudly in search of American folk food traditions for *Natural History*. And the very best purveyors of burgers and 'cue really did deserve the acclaim I could give them, and this, in a world of nauseatingly bad national

chains and commercial rip-offs like Big Bob's, was an honest blow
for the stubborn practitioners of quality, tradition and, sometimes,
worthwhile innovation, a blow I was happy to strike.

The travel itself was exhilarating in its weird mix of grinding
discomfort, discovery of the delicious treasure previously uncon-
sidered by the ballyhoo industry and bright contrasts between the
grit of the subject and the corporate cash that subtended my efforts.

Take the Texas leg of the barbecue story. It started in utter
expense-account comfort at the Four Seasons in Austin, with a
vague plan to drive on to the Hill Country, a collection of small
towns settled chiefly by German immigrants, where barbecued
beef was the local religion and a lure for gastrotourists of all levels
of income and refinement. That plan gained sharper focus over
dinner in Austin with Louis Black, the cofounder and editor of the
Austin Chronicle as well as the cofounder of the South by Southwest
Festival. A native of Teaneck, New Jersey, who had been imbibing
local lore and culture since his student days at the University of
Texas, Black gave me a list of places, and I went to them all.

Fortunately, we got to Lockhart, the very best of the Hill Country barbecue towns, early in the day, before too many fatty brisket
slices dulled our judgment. By then, on outings in Tennessee, Alabama and several other states famous for their brand of 'cue, I'd
already stuffed myself with smoky renditions of pulled pork and
pork shoulder, ribs and other slow-cooked animal parts, in dozens
of self-consciously down-home joints with rolls of paper towel-
ing standing tall on vertical holders, instead of napkins. So by the
time I rolled into little, semigentrified Lockhart (pop. 14,237), I
was, if not jaded, at least not remotely energized by the prospect of
another plate of meat collapsing from its own weight among piles
of cole slaw, baked beans or other canonical "sides," followed by
banana pudding bulked out with Nilla wafers.

It was, therefore, thoroughly remarkable that the beef brisket at Kreuz woke me up and changed my perspective on barbecue pretty completely. It was a paradigm shift.

Kreuz, pronounced *Krites* and referred to in some quarters as the Church of Krites, is, compared to the gaudy, shameless, huck-stering, media-fawning baroque of Big Bob Gibson's or Mike Mills's 17th Street Bar & Grill in Murphysboro, Illinois, a monas-tic retreat. Kreuz does not sell sides. It has no special sauces (like the one so fetishized by Mike Mills that he likes to say he'd have to kill anyone who got hold of the recipe). In fact, it has no standalone sauces at all.

Smitty's Market in Lockhart is even purer and plainer. In my first bite of brisket at Smitty's, the smokiness was so strong it changed my idea forever of what barbecue could be. This style of heavily smoked beef may take some getting used to, but for me it is the zenith of the 'cue universe. That doesn't mean I don't love the pork barbecue other regions excel in. But Smitty's is a temple of the pristine, a shaded cave of making, with its stark, black steel—doored smokers and taciturn pit men who stand in the heat of the post-oak logs, pull out a piece of brisket and ask you if you want it sliced from the lean or the fatty end. I went for the fatty and didn't mind that Smitty's is really not a restaurant but a specialized meat market. Out front, there is a shockingly bright, pathetic excuse for a dining room, which only makes the crepuscular Hades in the sooty pit area, which some genius implanted into an old brick brewery, seem even more wonderfully infernal. When you go through the door from this dusk to the fluorescent glare and the crappy tables of Smitty's dining room, the transition is something like the shock Plato tells us his cave dwellers experienced when they emerged into the sun.

There are many things you might want to tell other people about Smitty's, but the smokiness in the meat is the main lesson I learned that morning, and the thin pink line at the edge of each slice, which is the sign of the oaky gauntlet it has run for a dozen hours or more.

We drove on for the rest of the day, from the Hill Country, in central Texas,* all the way north into the tornado belt of Oklahoma, taking in that region's barbecue specialties, hickory-smoked brisket, bologna and pickled mixed vegetables, at black places like Leo's in Oklahoma City and Wilson's in Tulsa.

Eventually, in the warm months of 2007, I followed the barbecue trail through twelve states and came away convinced that the bigger the hoopla, the more acute the disappointment. At the huge festival on the banks of the Mississippi called Memphis in May, I got sunburned and burned in general at the insulting scam, in which dozens of "famous" barbecue teams compete with their "famous" sauces and meats from their portable pits, but the thousands of ticket holders rarely get a taste of that "famous" meat, which is not for sale but prepared for the elite palates of the judges alone. We regular folk were invited to look on with our tongues out.

On a tip from a Memphis native—Edward Felsenthal, Tom Weber's boss at the *Journal*—we drove to tiny Mason, Tennessee, east of Memphis, to Bozo's, which is to barbecue pork as Smitty's is to beef. At Bozo's, you don't need to sauce up the perfect quills of pork shoulder. Outside this unassuming family operation, a lonely whistling freight train rumbled by. The bright lights of the high-

---

* As many readers pointed out, Lockhart and the other barbecue centers we visited near Austin are not, technically, in the Hill Country. The Hill Country proper stretches west from Austin to the northern suburbs of San Antonio. But the name has been misapplied to the Texas barbecue belt, just as New York's borscht belt has appropriated the Catskill label, which, strictly speaking, should be applied only to the true Catskill range way to the north of the "Jewish Alps" of Sullivan County. But only a tiresome pedant would complain about these harmless confusions so deeply entrenched in everyday usage. When those clucking letters came in setting me straight about the Hill Country, I thought about similar outcries that occur every time someone dares to identify a tomato as a vegetable. I am, of course, aware that tomatoes, like other fleshy, seed-bearing plant parts, are known to botanists as fruits.

security prison next door cast an ominous shadow on the humble former farmhouse. Within, all was good cheer restrained by the confident reserve that results from knowing you can pull pork so that each strand comes away long and perfect, like hanks of moist beige yarn.

This was the Memphis style at its apogee, thirty-five miles from Graceland, and all the other sights and sounds of downtown Memphis. Bozo's does not serve ribs. Don't ask for brisket, either. In this shrine of the shoulder of the sow, aficionados know that "barbecue" signifies only one cut of meat, from high on the hog.

But you don't have to stay in the backwaters of the South to find very good barbecue, because the appetite for this food has spawned fine pits all over the land—at Slows, across from Detroit's derelict rail station; at the East Coast Grill in Cambridge, Massachusetts; and in Manhattan, at a clone of Kreuz called Hill Country.

Only in California did I strike out completely in my search for great barbecue. This was unfortunate (but perhaps an inevitable result of the overwhelming importance of Hispanic and Asian food in California's vernacular food world) but I didn't waste much of my time there. I sampled undistinguished 'cue in South Central Los Angeles, boarded a redeye and flew back to New York.

Even before the barbecue piece appeared in the paper, it made a splash. The online edition of the *Journal* was posted a bit before the newsprint broadsheet arrived at subscribers' doors and desks. The paper attached an e-mail address to the piece so that readers could "interact." And they did—many more than had ever written in about one of my articles in the pre-Internet era.

Reader reaction was only part of the Internet's effect on me. As late as 2002, when I left my editing job at the *Journal*, the telephone had still been a major tool of research and professional communication. When I returned to the paper in 2006, I did almost everything online. Instead of wasting time on hold with reservationists,

I booked online through OpenTable. To get a preliminary idea of where to eat in an unfamiliar town, I consulted sites from Zagat to Yelp. Since many of my early columns were, in effect, about food trends as they emerged on restaurant menus, I would search the cybercosmos for additional examples of a new ingredient or recipe I'd noticed by accident while dining out on assignment.

For example, I was surprised to see snails in a pasta dish at an Italian restaurant in New York. In my previous experience, snails had always been escargots, that cliché of retro French bistros—usually canned, swimming in garlic butter and, often, inserted into shells not originally their own.

Was the humble snail creeping out of this tired presentation? Were diners around the country confronting what might be called free-gliding snails, snails without shells and garlic butter, snails in omelets or snails with lobster?

They were. A quick Web search turned up creative snail dishes on several menus, including one at the innovative new regional Bluestem, in Kansas City. I flew in for dinner and, using the snail "trend" as a pretext, gave national attention to an excellent, quietly locavore outpost of first-rate food in the heart of the heart of the country. The headline: SLOW FOOD.

The discovery of the Internet as a powerful trend-spotting tool was a dangerous development. It was difficult not to believe that you could prove anything if you surfed diligently enough, even if that evidence was lurking somewhere on the 75,987th page of a Google search.

For the culture of dining and cookery, the Internet changed everything, just as it did in every other corner of life. But for a restaurant critic trying to operate nationally with no research assistant or other backup (and for those four years, I was the only food critic writing regularly and systematically in a major newspaper about the entire country, with frequent forays abroad), the Internet was indispensable, if only because almost every restaurant worth writing about had a website with hours, phone numbers, e-mail access for reservations, street addresses, maps and, most of all, menus. In the pre-Internet world of the early 1970s, I went out to eat without any clear idea of what would be available. The restaurant PR industry rarely sent me a menu, just vapid and information-free press releases. So I was reduced to stealing menus, as Craig Claiborne had advised, just to have a record of the meal. Those menus were also helpful to me as a reporter. When I wanted to interview a chef for a feature article, I could look at his menu and decide what dishes I would ask him to demonstrate for me.

Especially in dealing with Sichuan chefs who spoke no English, it was very useful to be able to point to a dish on the menu. I rapidly got used to arriving unannounced in a restaurant I had reviewed—calling ahead was useless, since the person at the other end could barely understand a simple request for a reservation. I would bring with me a set of measuring spoons and a measuring cup. Then I had to insert myself into the cooking process, so that I could get accurate measurements for the recipe I wanted to publish. Uncle Lou, the Sichuan master chef, was one of many cooks who suffered with friendly bewilderment the intrusions of the young man from the *Times* thrusting little spoons into his *mise-en-place*.

But that was the only way I could take home a recipe of his hot spicy shrimp (and all the other dishes from Sichuan I was the first person to publish in English). Then the scribbled notes would get transcribed into proper recipe form, with a list of ingredients at the top, in the order they were used in the numbered directions below, which were always followed by a "yield," the number of servings you would get from the recipe.

Even in 1971, this recipe format had a whiff of the home-economics test kitchen about it. Julia Child had already evolved a more complex and comprehensible format, but I still prefer its straightforward structure, especially since I worked with it every day at the *Times.*

I did my own testing then, at home. If I made mistakes, they would be my own. Also, my kitchen was a much more realistic arena for testing recipes for readers who, like me, were cooking with conventional ranges, instead of the professional-style Garland behemoth in the *Times* test kitchen.

The recipe testing made me a much better cook. And I discovered that I enjoyed the time at the stove. I especially loved baking bread, with its long periods of waiting while the yeast did its magic in the dough. I would read a novel or write a piece. Then I'd have a better loaf than I could easily buy in that era (so hard to imagine now) before artisanal bakers had put crusty sourdough on the shelves of national supermarket chains.

By 2006, anyone who wanted a classic baguette or a ciabatta could just buy one in the neighborhood. I did not mind not needing to bake myself, since I was really too busy traveling for the *Journal.* And I certainly did not regret not needing to steal menus anymore. The last time I'd wished I had stuck one in my pocket was at dinner at Pierre Gagnaire's Paris three-star establishment in the mid-1990s, where I'd found it tiresome to be taking notes in the dark during an almost comically intricate multicourse meal. I asked for a menu to keep. The captain refused point-blank and, only after I insisted, very grudgingly agreed to make a photocopy. They had a Xerox machine in the back office. Today, like virtually every restaurant of consequence, Pierre Gagnaire has a website with a menu on it. No one any longer needs to beg or steal a copy, or try to write down a jawbreaker dish name like that recent Gagnaire soup extraordinaire: *Consommé de boeuf au Banyuls, salsifis caramélisés, topinambours à la moutarde de Cramone et glace de maïs* (beef consommé with Banyuls wine, caramelized salsifys [oyster plants], Jerusalem artichokes with *mostarda di Cremona,* Italian candied fruit in mustard-oil syrup, and corn ice cream).

As a twenty-first-century food critic, I rarely ate a meal I hadn't been able to plan in advance at the computer. And when I paid by credit card in the restaurant, the computer-generated receipt came with a separate little printout of every dish I'd ordered. And no waiter ever flinched if I pulled out a small digital camera and took a picture of a dish, which I could e-mail to my editor from the table for later publication.

Of all these brave new efficiencies, e-mail was by far the most important. I could file my stories instantaneously and receive back edited copy wherever I happened to be. Compare that to the way reporters filed to the *New York Times* from the field in 1971. We would call a number in New York and read our articles to a monitored recording machine, spelling every name and unusual word. And in many cases, the next contact we had with our dispatches was when we read them in the paper. Garbles and mistakes were inevitable.

The computer and e-mail changed all that.

What had happened, from my perspective as a classicist, was the elimination of scribal error. For the first time since the invention of writing, nothing needed to be copied. The text, once it had been saved as a digital document, could be moved into print or disseminated electronically with no risk of human errors being introduced, as they always had been since antiquity, first by scribes who had hand-copied every book until Gutenberg, after whom the job of copying was shifted to type compositors and their successors at the keyboards of linotype machines.

But with the computer, the blurring chain of transmission came to an end. The author's version was, in principle, immutable and eternal. It could be revised, but the age-old need for the error-making scribe, the meddling keystroker, the secretary generating mistakes again and again through laboriously retyped versions of a letter or a chapter was finished. And no one would ever need to cut carbons again or risk the loss of years of work when a manuscript got left in a cab or burned.

I loved the computer and I loved e-mail even more. Especially because it brought me mail from readers who told me things I didn't know. In their passion to set me straight or rant at me, they often broadened my scope and—the best of them, anyway—gave me ideas for new columns. And a columnist is always in need of ideas for the next column.

At Cranbrook School, in the vaulted dining room designed by Eliel Saarinen that we called the carbohydrate cathedral, the standard grace before the meal was "Make us ever mindful of the needs of others." In the reverberating din of three hundred boys reciting that prayer, some of us would say instead, "Make us needful of the minds of others." A juvenile quip, sure, but also an essential precept for all intellectual activity, one acutely necessary for a hack with space to fill every day (or in my case at the *Journal*, every other week).

After the barbecue cover, I received a helpful e-mail from Charles Perry of Birmingham, Alabama, who claimed most persuasively that I had unaccountably neglected the barbecued ribs of his region.

He wrote: "In a small town outside of Birmingham, Cahaba Heights (now part of the suburb of Vestavia), there lies a dark, carbon encrusted pit . . . surrounded by a quaint brick structure with concrete slab floors and grease stained walls from years of preparing some of the best slow-cooked swine one could ingest. Miss Myra's BBQ awaits your review . . ."

Who could resist such a pitch?

Perry and his friend Jordan Brooks took me to three extraordinary shrines of the barbecue art: one in Birmingham and two in Tuscaloosa, an hour away, where they both had graduated from the University of Alabama in the previous century. Of the three 'cue temples we visited, Miss Myra's Pit Bar-B-Q, in Birmingham, was easily the furthest from those shacks in the piney woods of Dixie where this most durable and rib-sticking of our regional cuisines was born. For example, it has a sculpture collection, a veritable museum of swine art consisting of hundreds of effigies of the genus *Sus* in all its pink, piggy majesty. This enthusiasm for porcine imagery didn't prevent the cheerful staff at Miss Myra's from subjecting the racks of a multitude of hogs to a moist indirect heat that produced ribs better than any I had eaten anywhere up until that moment. Miss Myra's also turned out a sublime barbecued chicken and served white sauce (spicy mayo with vinegar).

We pressed on toward Tuscaloosa and the University of Alabama campus, holy ground for my hosts. "Can't you feel your pulse quicken?" Perry asked me when we were still twenty miles away. Once there, we drove around the campus, stopping at the football stadium. "You'll want to take your shoes off now," Brooks announced. He was only half kidding. We paid our respects to full-length life-size statues of all the Alabama football coaches who'd had national championships, notably Paul "Bear" Bryant, in coat, tie and fedora, looking stern.

Then, like thousands of students and alumni, we went to Dreamland for ribs. The restaurant was founded in Tuscaloosa in 1958 by the aptly named John "Big Daddy" Bishop. On football Saturdays, Dreamland loyalists wait two and three hours to be served in this small but densely decorated unofficial adjunct of the university athletic department. The ribs are worth waiting for. Hickory gives them a milder smokiness than the post oak used in Texas, so Dreamland's pit turns out a subtler taste of fire with peppy seasoning. And there is no white-boning; the ribs pull off the rack without falling off the bone, the classic indication of ideal doneness. Getting ribs to that point requires constant diligence and lots of poking around in a hot pit.

The best place to witness this precise cooking was at Archibald's, in a nondescript location across from a pallet factory in nearby Northport. Archibald's was, and I say this with respect, a real, mythic 'cue shack. The green clapboard walls weren't falling down, but the boards were definitely not plumb. The pit was a concrete-block affair attached directly to the small building. And a stack of wood sat a few feet away.

"You know the barbecue is good if the woodpile is bigger than the restaurant," Perry said.

The ribs were very crisp outside, moist inside. Betty Archibald served them in a pool of orange, vinegary hot sauce. Their taste stood up nicely to the sauce. The side dishes here were literally on the side—of the wall next to the pit. Little bags of munchies. The ribs were what counted.

All three of us marveled at Mrs. Archibald's intensity. She kept opening the pit's door and fussing with racks of ribs, moving them around with a pitchfork.

That kind of hands-on, personal, obsessively careful cooking also produced my number one choices for the hot dog and hamburger covers Tom Weber had commissioned me to write for the *Journal*. Both Speed's, the Boston hot dog genius, and Miss Ann, the hamburger dowager empress of Atlanta, operated on the smallest possible scale, following their own special method for improving on dishes served with less distinction elsewhere on a frighteningly vast scale. They both shunned publicity and showed no interest in maximizing profits or branching out. (Miss Ann was positively bitter about the assault of customers my article brought her.) I sniffed them out from various friends' tips and from persuasive recommendations on the Internet. Similar advice led me to dozens of other little places, but Speed and Miss Ann stood out, way out and above the others.

Speed sold his hot dogs when it pleased him in Newmarket Square, which is not some historic New England green space on the model of the Boston Common but a triangular parking lot surrounded by bleak wholesale food warehouses in the unfrilly purlieu of Roxbury. His "restaurant" was a food truck with a makeshift kitchen in it. Speed himself was a quietly gregarious older man, said to have been a fast-talking DJ in the day, whence the nickname he goes by instead of his real name, Ezra Anderson. He was friendly and leaked his secret recipe to me with a conspiratorial half-wink.

Speed confided that he coaxed such wonderful flavor out of a run-of-the-mill commercial dog by marinating the dog in apple cider and brown sugar. Then he grilled it over charcoal. Actually, this octogenarian entrepreneur let his young apprentices handle the dogs under his watchful eye. They also toasted the buns. By legend, the piquant relish he supplied along with raw onions and beanless chili to pack into his split franks was another Speed treasure made by the man himself.

Speed was palsy and open; Miss Ann ran her little shop like a tough schoolmarm. When it was full, customers had to wait on the porch until those already seated finished up and left.

Ann's Snack Bar occupied an unpromising lot on a broken-down industrial stretch of highway. Miss Ann worked alone at her grill, patting each ample patty lightly as she set it down to cook. Her masterpiece, the "ghetto burger," was a two-patty cheeseburger tricked out with bacon that she had tended closely in a fryolator.

Observing Miss Ann in action would have been enough of a show to take a visitor's mind off his hunger. But while the lady demonstrated the extreme economy of motion of a superb short-order cook, she simultaneously carried on a running dialogue of lightly sassy repartee with customers she knew.

In mid-sentence, Miss Ann would dust your almost-ready patties with "seasoned salt" tinged red from cayenne pepper. It looked like a mistake, too much, over the top. But when you got your ghetto burger in its handsomely toasted bun envelope, you regretted doubting her for one second. The big burgers stood up fine to the spice. And they just barely fit in your mouth.

Miss Ann. Speed. Betty Archibald. Did I pick them because they were colorful loners at the margins of mainstream America? Sticking a finger in the eye of the fast-food industry was never my goal, but it was inevitable that I would prefer idiosyncratic, independent cooks with a special spin on the most widely cooked dishes in American culinary life. Interestingly, all three of them turned out to be black and elderly. Each time I'd embarked on one of those cover stories, I'd been convinced the project was bogus. I couldn't imagine that even the best burger or ribs or dogs would be worth the kind of hype a cover piece in the Saturday *Journal*'s Pursuits section would require. And then Speed and Ann and Betty Archibald would turn the whole silly business of claiming I'd found the nation's finest examples of its favorite foods into a crusade for recognizing talent and craft.

As I traveled more and more as a restaurant critic, I saw that ambitious restaurants had sprung up in almost every city. Yes, the density of New York's restaurant culture surpassed that of other cities, but my experiences on the road persuaded me that the dining life in Chicago offered more adventure and excitement. And that Las Vegas was a far more interesting food scene than what a discriminating traveler might encounter in Los Angeles or San Francisco. Even more surprising were the dozens of remarkable, sophisticated restaurants I started finding in "flyover" towns like St. Paul and Boulder and even Duluth.

No can say with certainty how what was not so long ago a gastronomic wasteland between the coasts turned into a happy hunting ground for the sophisticated eater. But it seems clear that, starting in the late sixties, a critical mass of information and training kept growing. Food-minded tourists came home and began to cook the food they'd tasted on its home ground, guided by authentic and practicable recipes that put the foods of France (Julia Child), Mexico (Diana Kennedy), Morocco (Paula Wolfert), Sichuan (Ellen Schrecker and, much later, Fuchsia Dunlop), Italy (Marcella Hazan and many others), Greece (Diane Kochilas), Spain (Penelope Casas) and the Middle East (Claudia Roden) within reach of home cooks. Professionals could train seriously in various schools around the country, most of which hadn't existed in 1970.

Many of the most ambitious students spent time in European restaurants as apprentices to famous chefs, an opportunity that had barely existed in the old days. When they returned home, the hugely enlarged network of quality restaurants gave them interesting work and a chance to burnish their résumés.

Grant Achatz, born in 1974, grew up in a family restaurant business before attending the Culinary Institute of America, which landed him a job at the French Laundry, from which he rose to be top chef at the pathbreaking Trio in Chicago, a stepping stone to his even more radical, molecular-gastronomic megasuccess Alinea, also in Chicago.

Najat Kaanache, born in 1978 in Spain of Moroccan parents who worked in agriculture, abandoned a career in acting for culinary school in Holland, where she apprenticed with François Geurds, a former sous-chef under Heston Blumenthal at the three-star Fat Duck, outside London. To consolidate her training, she arranged *stages* under Achatz, René Redzepi of Noma, in Copenhagen, and with Ferran Adrià at El Bulli, north of Barcelona.

That almost all of her mentors are household names, at least in food-conscious households around the world, is a remarkable fact entirely apart from this young woman's ability to navigate so sure-footedly in a global network of superstars. Still more remarkable is that this network exists and that its biggest names transcend national borders, influence one another and reinforce the culture of food that has fostered their careers.

At the weeklong celebration of Charlie Trotter's twentieth anniversary as Chicago's most honored chef, in 2007, six other world-beating chefs cooked the main banquet. Adrià was in the kitchen, as was Blumenthal, who stole the show with a pictorial and auditory shore dinner. He hid iPod Shuffles in whelk shells that sat next to a delicious seafood mixture on each of eighty guests' plates, so that they could listen to sounds of the sea on earphones while they ate a complex seafood medley bathed in seafood foam.

This confraternity of stellar cooks was, even for the twenty-first century, a notable gathering of globalized culinary celebrity. But it was only the most glamorous example of a less public networking that connects the alert kitchens of our day, most concretely in the form of hot new recipes that spread around the cybersphere instantaneously and then end up in slightly varied versions on plates far from their origins.

In 1977, I caught an early glimpse of this on a tour of Michelin three-stars in France, where virtually every menu offered some form of early asparagus in oblong boxes of puff pastry. I was tempted to sleuth out which chef had started this mini-vogue, but what mattered was that all of them were so aware of this new idea and that they all had latched onto it that same month. And that was before the Internet.

By 2007, dozens and dozens of chefs, not just the mandarins of the French Michelin, were blithely appropriating the newest wrinkle, from the most distant kitchens, instantaneously, in cyberspace.

When Anne Burrell, a protégée of Mario Batali's, opened Centro Vinoteca across the street from me in Greenwich Village, among the Italianate small-plate dishes on her menu was an intriguing pasta, a single large ravioli with a liquid egg yolk concealed inside. In the restaurant's basement kitchen, I observed as a meticulous fellow called Humberto rolled out a long, thin layer of dough for the steroidal ravioli and cut out three-inch disks from it with a sort of cookie cutter. Onto them he spread a mixture of ricotta and Parmesan cheese. Then he cracked an egg, separated the yolk from the white and gingerly deposited a perfect sun of a yolk on the cheese. A second disk of dough went on top and was pressed in place to make a single large raviolo ("ravioli" is the plural), or, to be more exact, a *raviolone* (the last syllable, an Italian "augmentative," implies bigness beyond the normal) with a raw yolk inside.

After a brief (say, three-minute) poaching in gently simmering water, the dough was barely cooked, as was the still-liquid, ready-to-burst-on-fork-contact yolk. When the *raviolone* was served upstairs, Burrell would emerge from the open kitchen to shave an ounce of white truffle over it.

Even without that pricey fillip, her delicate egg surprise was an established winner well before Ms. Burrell brought it to Seventh Avenue South. Long before she tried her hand at making one, this witty dish had helped earn the reputation of the great Italian restaurant San Domenico, at Imola, near Bologna.

From there, it had spread not only to my corner but across the country. Diners had reported encounters at Boston's Prezza and at Prima Ristorante in Boulder, Colorado. Rising star chef Steve Mannino was stuffing his pasta pouches with quail eggs and wild mushrooms at the Las Vegas Olives, in the Bellagio Hotel. And at classy Fifth Floor, in San Francisco, before it got a Michelin star, Chef Melissa Perello had put her signature on the dish with a duck egg, porcini mushrooms, peas and serrano ham.

In another example of fast-moving recipes, at just about the time the egg *raviolone* was making the rounds, the lucky gourmet could find the same elegant butter-poached lobster recipe adorning tables at the French Laundry and at Barbara Lynch's No. 9 Park, on Beacon Hill in Boston.

Circulating apprentices, food blogs, tweets and other Internet channels all were playing a role in the spread of food ideas. But the most powerful multiplier of food news and stoker of chefs' ideas and reputations was undoubtedly television. It started with Julia Child's black-and-white series *The French Chef,* which made her the first star of noncommercial TV. A few serious cooks flourish on television today, but it is impossible to imagine Julia making a career in the same shrill, crass universe reigned over by Paula Deen and others who didn't make any major culinary mark before television brought them fame. Deen, exhaustingly exuberant, was, when I checked in 2006, on the air sixteen times a week and being watched by a total of seven million viewers as she demonstrated conventional recipes drawn from traditional southern cooking.

The lunch I ate at Ms. Deen's equally popular Savannah restaurant, the Lady & Sons, wasn't any good. But the crowd around us in that multistoried eatery that serves hundreds of meals daily looked happy enough, ratifying their fandom with knife and fork. Would they have been as happy eating better versions of the same regional food at a nearby tavern called Moon River Brewing Company (after the hit tune by Savannahian Johnny Mercer)? Would they have been as thrilled as I was by superb renditions and improvisations on these dishes at the Beard-award-winning Elizabeth's, down the road? I'd like to think so.

Someday, I want to test the idea that everyone is born with a good palate. I would conduct the experiment on my own TV show, a culinary remake of *The Millionaire*. I'd find a lucky couple at a fast-food restaurant and whisk them off to some five-star temple, where I'd let them eat their way through the menu. At the Lady & Sons, I fantasized for a bit about that couple's purrs of pleasure, until the reality show around me—equal parts *Six Feet Under* (dead victuals) and *CSI: Crime Scene Investigation* (unsightly victims of criminal cooking)—preempted my attention.

I walked swiftly by the tired buffet of southern fried chicken and soulful veggies. At the bar, I ate soggy fried green tomatoes and munched fitfully on a doughy biscuit while the couple next to me drank their meal and left with cocktails in hand for a trolley tour of the settings of John Berendt's best-selling account of decadent Savannah, *Midnight in the Garden of Good and Evil.*

My main course consisted of stringy crab molded into an uncrisp cake. It reminded me of what I'd known all along: there's no business like show business.

Deen on the tube is a superior cook to the Paula Deen whose actual food you eat in Savannah. Her recipes are perfectly respectable versions of southern home cooking. The entire stick of butter she likes to drop into the pan with a lascivious leer is no cruder than the river of *beurre* Joël Robuchon works into the mashed potatoes that helped vault him to the top of contemporary French cooking. Deen's rise from humble beginnings as a purveyor of lunches hand-delivered by her sons is a winning yarn, no less convincing because it is true.

The trouble isn't in the star, but in her success—that her restaurant is an insult to the very fan loyalty it sells out. The place is just too big. When Berendt wrote, in an introduction to *The Lady & Sons Savannah County Cookbook* in 1998, that the earlier restaurant offered "a short course in the meaning of Southern cooking—the flavors, the ambience, indeed the very *heart* of Southern cooking," it had eighty-five seats. The Lady & Sons lost its soul when it moved, in 2003, into its 330-seat, fifteen-thousand-square-foot dining headquarters.

I experienced the gracious heart of southern cooking in Savannah, at Elizabeth Terry's turn-of-the-century Greek Revival mansion just south of downtown. There the cheese biscuits had just come from the oven, nicely browned. There the crab cakes were nicely crisped and contained pieces of crabmeat that looked as if they came from crabs, not an industrial processor.

In the dining room, fitted out with Windsor chairs and trompe l'oeil murals of flowers and household objects, local food tradition was honored with such presentations as spicy shrimp and country ham in redeye gravy, flanked by wedges of fried grits standing on edge like sentinels. This fine thing, like the equally fine crab cake, cost $13.95, less than a dollar more than the crab cake at the Lady & Sons. You could, of course, spend considerably more on main courses at Elizabeth's. The grouper special, an imaginative fantasia of local fish and vegetables, ran $33.95. Yet it wasn't egregiously pricier than the Lady & Sons' beef-and-tomato pie ($24.99).

The only things missing at Elizabeth's were the pizzazz and lugubrious self-promotion of the Lady & Sons. The eponymous Elizabeth and her two daughters haven't, so far as they have let on in the limited publicity they have released, suffered like Paula Deen from agoraphobia, been robbed at gunpoint or rallied from a divorce to find middle-aged romance with a bearded boatman.

I doubt, in other words, that food television, in its flamboyant new mode, is doing much for the encouragement of good taste and culinary knowledge in its public of millions.

Exposure on TV has surely benefited the careers of authentic talents such as Mario ("Molto Mario") Batali, while the young chefs who prosper in the preposterous cooking competitions staged for television can leverage their ability to concoct a winning dish out of seven never previously combined ingredients into financial backing for a restaurant. But real creativity in the kitchen is not a stunt carried off under terrible time pressure. Indeed, creativity hasn't been a central notion in the historical narrative of the kitchen, even, or perhaps especially not, in the development of haute cuisine, until the current period of chef worship and perfervid admiration of novelty.

I saw the effect of TV food shows at its worst at a wildly popular new restaurant in Chicago, Girl & the Goat, created by a *Top Chef* winner named Stephanie Izard. Girl & the Goat's menu is a catalog of dishes straining for originality, a chaos of strong-flavored ingredients that knock one another out: kohlrabi salad with toasted almonds, *and* pear, *and* ginger dressing; or fennel potato-rice crepes with butternut squash, *and* shiitake kimchi, *and* mushroom jus.

In 2009, I got a chance to see a real top chef invent a dish, and it was a very different, careful improvisation. With over twenty Michelin stars worldwide, Joël Robuchon is arguably the planet's most successful restaurateur. Three of his many branches have the red guide's highest ranking, three stars: one in Macao, one in Tokyo and one in Las Vegas, in the MGM Grand Hotel.

Four times a year, Robuchon visits Nevada to redesign the menu at this fabulous, small pinnacle of gastronomy. I arranged to meet him there and watched him tweak a crab recipe for his new spring menu.

The world's most decorated chef was drinking a Diet Coke as he entered the immaculate kitchen, followed by a small posse of underchefs. He inspected a small circular tin of osetra caviar and then pulled apart an Alaskan king crab the size of a puppy.* "Where is the coral?" he asked, setting off nervous scurrying and

---

* I could not help remembering the urban legend about a gigantic king crab being flown from Anchorage to Paris on Air France, destined for a new home at the Aquarium de Paris. A galley steward discovered the creature in his refrigerator. He steamed it and served it to his first-class passengers.

whispers. Coral, the red, deeply flavorful female crab's egg mass he needs for the sauce, was found in another big crab. The kitchen had previously prepared cooked meat from king, Dungeness and blue crabs, which Robuchon tasted in different mixtures, pulling out samples with his fingers. In the end, he decided on a mélange of king and Dungeness.

"For me it's all about the texture," he said.

The new spring menu was centered on shellfish. "Americans really love shellfish," he told me, as if to congratulate me and more than 300 million other compatriots for our good taste.

He went on to build his new dish by layering the crab mixture with strips of yellow-brown Santa Barbara sea urchin, which he extracted from a neat pile. The crustaceans were only the beginning. Minced raw white cauliflower was also a major ingredient. It would lurk within the crabmeat mix as a stealth carrier of crunch, which Robuchon said he believes makes this dish a no-grain marine cousin of tabbouleh, the ancient Near Eastern salad based on bulgur wheat and mint. To carry the edible metaphor all the way, the chef added mint to his crab creation.

The diner who ordered this crab-and-cauliflower "tabbouleh" at the start of the 2009 spring menu received a small caviar tin, inside which only black osetra eggs were visible. But when he attacked them with his fork, the action unearthed a chamber symphony of crab, cauliflower and mint, the faux tabbouleh concealed under the caviar emerged, and everything merged on the tongue in the most unexpected and beautiful way.

"I just had this idea in my head," Robuchon explained, without, of course, explaining anything.

On that same February visit, I returned to the jewel-box dining room adjoining but totally insulated from the MGM Grand's casino, for the restaurant's winter menu. No course included more than four ingredients, and the often surprising combinations did not war with one another. An egg yolk hid in an herb-flavored raviolo: there it was again, the San Domenico *raviolone,* raised a notch with a medley of black truffle shavings and orbs of baby spinach foam—two kinds of spherical shapes, one on a convex mount, the other in a concave container.

Then I got my favorite course, the frog leg fritter. This iconic food of France was presented as a single gobbet of flesh with a matchstick of bone sticking up as a handle—letting you pop the thing, with its crisp, bird's-nest coating, into your mouth, but only after you'd dredged it through teardrops of garlic cream and parsley puree, chaste reminders of the dish's origins in Provence.

I was equally amused and delighted to see how Robuchon ennobled the lowly turnip with candied chestnuts in a foie gras broth. The flavors and textures married as if centuries of trial and error had long since made the combination commonplace. Ditto for the very strange velvety soup of oats studded with toasted almond and red dots of chorizo juice—superior comfort chow pepped up with crunchy almond bits hiding in the porridge. Odd, too, and also magnificent was the "risotto" of soy shoots with lemon zest and chive.

Toward the end of the evening, the courses turned less fanciful. A piece of veal with a napoleon of vegetables and a natural herb gel preceded an exemplary bass, served unadorned except for its crisp skin and a dark red pool of sauce derived from verjuice, the acidic liquid pressed from unripe grapes. The breathtaking simplicity of these two main dishes only underlined how radical the earlier part of the meal had been. Then, just as I thought he was winding down, Robuchon at his trickiest conjured up a rococo assemblage called Le Coca.

As in cola.

This tribute to the chef's beloved soda consisted of a ginger mousse, an ice made from vodka and Coke, and something dark, a

Mr Sokolov and Guest

L'HIVER

~ Dîner du mardi 17 février 2009 ~
Imaginé par Joël Robuchon

La Pomme
une gelée rafraichie de noix de muscade voilée d'un filet d'huile d'olive extra vierge
Apple in a light gelée refreshed with nutmeg, drizzled with extra virgin olive oil

***

Le Caviar
lamelles de Saint-Jacques tiédies au zeste de citron vert, une infusion prise à la crème de chou-fleur, des fines graines de couscous iodé
Thin slices of warm scallops with lime zest, smooth cauliflower cream, Thin couscous and Oscetra caviar

L'Œuf
le jaune dans un ravioli imprimé d'herbes aux épinards petites pousses et copeaux de truffes noires
Egg yolk in an herb ravioli, baby spinach and black truffles

La Grenouille
la cuisse en fritot à la crème aillée et au coulis de persil
Crispy frog leg, garlic and parsley puree

Le Navet
escorté de châtaignes confites au jus, petite nage fleurie aux aromates et foie gras
Turnip and confit chesnuts in a aromatic broth with foie gras

Les Crustacés
la langoustine truffée et cuite en ravioli à l'étuvée de choux vert,
le homard rôti à la citronnelle et curry,
l'oursin au fumet de fenouil
Truffle langoustine ravioli with chopped cabbage, lemon grass roasted lobster with vegetable Semolina, sea urchin with fennel broth

L'Avoine
veloutée aux amandes torréfiées et aux sucs de chorizo
Wild-oat velouté with roasted almonds and chorizo

Le Bar
cuit en peau aux cinq épices, avec une sauce au verjus
Pan-fried sea bass with the skin and five spices, served with verjus sauce

Le Veau
en côte au plat avec un jus gras et escorté de taglierinis de légumes au pistou
Sautéed veal chop with natural jus, vegetable and basil taglierinis

Les Pousses de Soja
cuites comme un risotto aux zestes d'agrumes et ciboulette
Soy beans cooked risotto style with lemon zests and chives

***

Le Coca
crème mousseuse au gingembre, granité de vodka-cola, bulle noire à la feuille d'or
Coca-Cola, ginger mousseline, vodka-cola granite and cola bubble with flag of gold

La Fuji
Fondante, parfumée au citron, glace yuzu aux airelles confites
Fuji apple confit in vanilla honey, yuzu ice cream and lemon marshmallow

***

Le Moka ou le Thé
escortés de mignardises

Joël Robuchon
RESTAURANT

bubble of Coca-Cola gelée crowned with gold. It was a grandiose joke, but Robuchon had taken the world's most famous industrial flavor and transmogrified it into a high culinary essence—still recognizably Coke, but also something way beyond.

That meal may have been the finest, and it definitely was one of the most creative, I ate in four years of free-range feeding at the summits of gastronomy. I was not surprised, since I had eaten in the same hidden Eden twice before. And in the course of many trips to Las Vegas, I had concluded that it offered the most intense opportunity to eat well in the United States and possibly in the world.

Robuchon had long ago given up on Paris for his fanciest flights. The economics of New York made it impossible for him to mount one of his "gastronomic" restaurants there. Even the New York branch of his more-relaxed Atelier chain folded in 2011. But in Las Vegas (as in that other gambling capital Macao, where he had won three stars with a similarly grand restaurant), he could count on support from the MGM Grand and from high rollers. This is why most of the big names in the restaurant pantheon have flocked to Vegas. Some, like Sirio Maccioni, of New York's Le Cirque, have merely knocked themselves off without knocking themselves out to achieve something great.

And yet the stigma that surrounds Sin City keeps some of my most food-minded acquaintances from going there.

In 2005, when a crazed foodie I know well decided to take six friends to dinner with her first Social Security check, she picked Chanterelle, the once-great Tribeca address that was cruising

---

Opposite: I ate my way through this menu from Joël Robuchon's three-star Michelin restaurant in Las Vegas in 2009, after interviewing the world's most honored chef in the little kitchen tucked inside the world's largest hotel, the MGM Grand. The menu included a fantasy dessert based, with a magician's sleight of hand, on Coca-Cola, Robuchon's workaday drink of choice.

toward its twilight. I suggested that if all eight of us pooled our Social Security checks, we could fly to Vegas, eat at Robuchon and fly home on the redeye, all without surrendering a dollar to the gambling industry or tainting ourselves with the vulgarity of the strip's carnival architecture.

We went to Chanterelle.

My final wallow in the Nevada desert as *Journal* food critic, in early 2010, coincided with the opening of MGM Mirage's City-Center, the sixty-nine-acre complex that nearly bankrupted Dubai. Gamblers were feeding the slots on the ground floor of the sixty-one-story Aria, the central property. Shoppers were trolling for glitz in Crystals, Daniel Libeskind's cavernous funhouse of a mall. There was major league art everywhere, by Robert Rauschenberg, Jenny Holzer, Frank Stella and, from Nancy Rubins, a monumental assemblage of multicolored boats moored together in the central traffic island. But most enticing for me was the lure of three "fine-dining" restaurants masterminded by three famous chefs.

How did I pick this trio out of the dozens so toothsomely described in CityCenter's advance publicity? They had to be outposts of very well-respected venues outside Vegas whose chefs had never worked there before. This may have been unfair to Michael Mina's American Fish or Julian Serrano's clever-looking celebration of Spain, named after himself, at Aria, or Wolfgang Puck's bistro inside Crystals. But food news is food news. And the arrival of three-star French master toque Pierre Gagnaire in North America, as well as the Clark County debuts of Chicago headliner Shawn McClain (Sage) and Masayoshi Takayama (Bar Masa and Shaboo), wizard of rawness at Masa in Manhattan's Time Warner Center, were the biggest news in this first season of CityCenter's struggling but apparently viable leviathan.

If, however, the only restaurant you landed in here was Takayama's Shaboo, you would have been on your Droid right away selling MGM Mirage short. Admittedly, Shaboo set the bar very high, even for the high-rollingest diner, in an economy unrecovered from the crash of 2008: $500 a person for a set but unpredictable meal, exclusive of wine service and tax. And even if you were willing to blow that kind of money on a blue-chip version of the traditional Japanese hot-pot cuisine, you also had to pass a credit check and not lose your nerve after two warnings, one from a reservationist and the other from a captain on the way to your table, about how pricey your indulgent dinner was going to be.

My wife, Johanna, and I had Shaboo, with its intimate fifty-two seats, all to ourselves, literally, except for a gallant staff of young women attendants, who helped us get the hang of pushing foie gras and other luxury oddments around in broth simmering over cool magnetic induction burners integrated into our table. We counted eight courses and many ingredients flown in at great cost from Japan. It may be that if we had been a couple of deeply experienced Japanese shabu-shabolators, this meal would have been some kind of pinnacle in our overcosseted gustatory lives. But as nonadepts at this form of mink-lined Zen cookery, we had a far finer time for far less liquidation of euroyen across the hall in the vast Aria lobby-atrium-casino at Sage.

Young McClain wasn't trying for a Guinness record as the world's priciest chef at Sage. But he may have deserved one for most eclectically attentive to high-end trends. Sage's subfusc elegance served as an all-purpose foil for food that represented his personal version of dishes that were hot all around the gastrostratosphere. There was a delicious foie gras crème brulée, a triumph of unctuous texture plays. Also, a slow-cooked "farm" egg, Iberico pork, toffee pudding—and a lot of other then-voguish ideas—were executed with assurance and even originality.

But what made this voyage westward really worth it was Twist, Pierre Gagnaire's bistro de luxe on the twenty-third floor of the discreet new Mandarin Oriental. I'd already eaten with mixed emotions at Gagnaire's flagship restaurant in Paris some years before, finding its food amazingly intricate but a muddle in the mouth, like a failed finger painting by an overly ambitious schoolkid: all those carefully managed ingredients melted together without any unifying taste drama. So I wasn't going to be an easy sell at Twist, despite its eagle's view of the lights of Vegas (a rare glimpse of the rest of the city from hermetic CityCenter) and the knowing assistance of a sommelier I trusted all the more since I had spied her at lunch at the Beard Award–nominated Thai restaurant Lotus of Siam, an unglamorous mecca for *Feinschmeckers* with a renowned German wine list in a grotty mall north of the Strip.*

Gagnaire hadn't totally abandoned his take-no-prisoners style at Twist, but his superego had gained control over his id. The foie gras tasting (four separate preparations, including a terrine with dried figs and toasted ginger bread; a custard with green lentils and grilled zucchini; a seared cube with duck glaze and fruit marmalade; and a croquette with trevicchio puree), served on a rectangular plate divided into four compartments, visually organized your sensations, and added up to an awe-inspiring and analytic tribute to the most overused expensive ingredient of all.

Gagnaire had also turned into an American locavore (at least in the airborne sense imposed on any cook in the agriculture-deprived environs of Las Vegas), sourcing his never-confined veal in Wisconsin from the estimable Strauss company. And to show what a great French cook can do with American lobster, Twist offered it poached in Sauternes with an impressive entourage of garnishes and a lobster bisque.

---

* Many people who have eaten there and know their galanga from their kaffir lime will tell you that Lotus of Siam in Vegas serves the best Thai food in North America. I agree; so I was downcast when the owners let themselves be persuaded to open a branch on lower Fifth Avenue in Manhattan that never came close to the heights of the dumpy original on Sahara Avenue before the Chutima family gave up the fight and retreated to Nevada.

It was Gagnaire and Robuchon's ability to adapt themselves to such an un-French, uniquely American setting that made their outposts in Nevada so special. If they had merely duplicated their brand of French luxury food in Las Vegas, that would have come off as sterile and smug, the way Alain Ducasse's first restaurant in New York did. But Gagnaire and Robuchon were able to reinvent themselves in the desert. They weren't cloning themselves, or conducting some stuffy *mission civilisatrice* among the heathen, as I felt Guy Savoy, another top Parisian chef, was doing at his restaurant down Las Vegas Boulevard, at Caesars Palace.

But even at their spectacular best, Robuchon and Gagnaire were pulling off a stunt. Las Vegas was not only not their home base, it was not, with the exception perhaps of a few native-born gastronomes, any of their customers' home bases either. The big gamblers the casinos call whales, the splurging conventioneers, the food lovers like me—we fly in for a few nights and don't come back for months or years. The pervasive mood of transience this creates is not the normal atmosphere that has historically nurtured great restaurants. Repeat customers, a sense of place, of rootedness—these are the missing ingredients in the epicure's paradise of Las Vegas.

But they are the core strengths of the ambitious restaurants I kept dropping in at in almost every American town I wrote about over those four years at the end of the first decade of the new millennium.

Behind the molecular-gastronomic smoke and mirrors at Alinea in Chicago was a backdrop of midwestern rootedness. Grant Achatz learned to cook at a family restaurant on the eastern shore of Lake Michigan, in Chicago's hinterland. He established himself first at Trio in Evanston, a Chicago suburb. Charlie Trotter is a Chicago native who lives down the street from his venerable restaurant, which was situated in a town house before Trotter

TROUT ROE parsnip, licorice, ginger

LEMONGRASS oyster, sesame, yuzu

CAULIFLOWER five coatings, three gels, cider

CHICKEN LIVER bacon, caramelized onion, vin santo

PEAR olive oil, black pepper, eucalyptus

COBIA tobacco, radish, cedarwood

URCHIN turnip, shiso, sudachi

TURBOT chamomile, shellfish, celery

SIX FLAVORS frozen

WAGYU BEEF maitake, smoked date, Blis Elixir

CONCORD GRAPE yogurt, mint, long pepper

SWEET POTATO brown sugar, bourbon, smoldering cinnamon

BACON butterscotch, apple, thyme

HOT POTATO cold potato, black truffle, butter

YUBA shrimp, miso, togarashi

KING CRAB popcorn, butter, curry

LAMB lemon, fennel, coffee aroma

BLACK TRUFFLE explosion, romaine, parmesan

CHESTNUT quince, chocolate, baked potato

TRANSPARENCY of raspberry, rose petal, yogurt

CRABAPPLE foie gras, brown sugar, sorrel

DRY SHOT pineapple, rum, cilantro

SPICE CAKE persimmon, rum, Ohio honeycomb

CHOCOLATE fig, olive, pine

DRY CARAMEL salt

ALINEA

1723 N Halsted   Chicago IL 60614   p 312.867.0110   f 312.482.8192
www.alinearestaurant.com   info@alinearestaurant.com

My dinner with Joel (and Maria) at Grant Achatz's modernist Alinea in
Chicago in early February 2007 included a helpful waiter who stood by
to explain this cryptic menu.

closed it in 2012. For many customers, Trotter's was a neighborhood eating place, a very good neighborhood place. The Morgan
Stanley financier Ray Harris ate at Trotter's more than three hundred times.

Most other cities in this era have restaurants with deep local
roots that serve food of "national" quality. "National," as I took to
using it in *Journal* reviews, meant that a restaurant in Des Moines
or Richmond, Virginia, was on a level with the best and most up-
to-date dining places on either coast, or in other acknowledged
food centers such as Chicago or Miami. And as I traveled around
America, I learned, with gratification and diminishing surprise,
just how many national places there were.

Take Sanford in Milwaukee. Like Charlie Trotter's, it was
established in a house, in a residential neighborhood, but the
neighborhood was nothing fancy; neither was the little house
where Sanford D'Amato and his wife, Angie, transformed a family
grocery store into a soberly elegant dining room more than twenty
years ago. Combining a cosmopolitan and up-to-date technique
with local ingredients, D'Amato applied his French technique
acquired at the Culinary Institute of America to roots cooking.
When I ate there in 2009, I ordered a timbale of smoked salmon
with rye cake, mustard mousseline and dill-pickled rutabaga. This
was high-low cuisine, with humble ingredients and flavors you
might have found in Milwaukee's most vernacular saloons.

But there was nothing plebeian about Sanford's menu, which
featured "green"* Strauss veal gently raised twenty miles to the
southwest in Franklin, Wisconsin. The night I was at Sanford,

* According to company literature, Strauss calves are "Free to Roam—never tethered or
raised in confinement. Raised on natural open pastures alongside mother & herd. Never
raised in feedlots. Unlimited access to mother's milk. Strictly vegetarian fed—never
receiving animal by-products. Never ever administered growth hormones. Never ever
administered antibiotics. Never experience the stress of industrialized farming."

this pampered meat appeared as a sous vide–tamed "17-hour" veal breast with escarole and pickled hedgehog mushrooms in a burnt-orange reduction. I finished the meal with a plate of five Wisconsin cheeses. Snow White goat cheddar and Carr Valley Billy Blue were far from the run-of-the-industrial-barn cheeses Wisconsin sells by the carload to the outside world.

You could hardly ask for a more harmonious blend of sauce making evolved from classic principles, local sourcing of ingredients and modernist methodology. The humble cut of veal breast illustrated perfectly why the sous vide technique has spread far and wide. Really just a precise form of low-temperature cooking in a water bath, sous vide softens tougher cuts of meat without the aggressive force of a traditional, high-temperature braise. It can also cook a salmon without drying it out, leaving the texture as smooth and as flavorful as sashimi but not raw.

Sous vide literally means "in a vacuum." The name has unnecessarily emphasized the fact that food is put in plastic bags, which then have the air sucked out of them, so that they cling tightly, protecting the food from the water in the bath but allowing essentially direct contact with the temperature of the water. Temperatures much lower than those of normal cooking preserved a freshness of flavor in the veal.

Later in 2008, I continued my heartland odyssey in Denver and Minneapolis, the two cities that hosted the party conventions, and made dining recommendations to the delegates.

I felt compelled to mention Denver's taxidermic showplace for regionally farmed game (elk and yak), the Buckhorn Exchange. But the "national" choice here was Restaurant Kevin Taylor in the chic Hotel Teatro, down the street from the convention center in downtown Denver's cultural and entertainment hub. I admired Taylor's treatments of red meat, the contrasting textures of tender Colorado dry-aged lamb sirloin and melting lamb belly dressed up with twice-baked eggplant, figs and pimenton peppers; the counterpoint of locally farmed bison sirloin and barbecued back ribs with black beans, cheddar corn grits and charred tomatillos; and the Snake River Farms Kobe rib eye and beef-cheek two-step, with tasty potatoes and a truffle-accented béarnaise sauce. But I really liked his olive oil–poached halibut cheek—big enough to make you hope he hadn't thrown away the rest of the fish. (Potato-crusted Alaskan halibut was available as a main course.)

At the other end of the social and sensory scale was Snooze, on a seedy block of pawnshops in Denver's ballpark neighborhood, a breakfast place serving coffee specially grown for it at a Guatemalan finca.

Minneapolis wasn't a patch on Denver, foodwise. The most original dining choice in the Twin Cities was on a drab block in plain-faced St. Paul, where I did my best to encourage Republican delegates to take their wives. If any of them did follow my advice and eat at Heartland, I am sure their power act didn't faze my waitress, who brought eight wineglasses at one swoop to a table near me in the storefront establishment's restrained dining room, with its open kitchen and rack of burly aluminum stockpots suspended above.

Heartland was locavorous on steroids, and I mean that kindly. Its Wisconsin elk tartare was a rich, dense, meticulously hand-chopped and not-at-all-gamy way to begin a splendid meal. I liked the menu so much I had a second starter: a subtly contrasting salad of chilled Canadian wheat berries and sweet corn with Donnay Dairy chèvre, microgreens and watercress pesto vinaigrette. I followed it with the midwestern mixed grill of Illinois fallow venison and Minnesota wild boar sausage, with Footjoy Farm flat beans, house-cured wild boar *guanciale* (jowl) and fresh ginger *glace de viande.*

Heartland was tucked away in a gray corner of the upper Midwest but cooking its heart out with top modern technique and bonhomie. As jumbo jets bound to shinier destinations flew overhead, the new food gospel was being preached here with expert ardor. Heartland literally inspired me, launched me on a long summer of exploration of flyover country to prove that savvy national places to eat abounded next to cornfields and in cities scorned by folks in New York County obsessed with snagging rezzies at Babbo.

In Omaha, bypassing Warren Buffett's local haunt Gorat's, where he washes down T-bones with Cherry Coke, I honed in on the rehabbed Old Market center, redolent of handmade soaps and other New Age gifts often found near fern bars. But in and around the exposed brick emporia were a couple of national-level watering holes, one hip and dreamy, La Buvette, the other, V. Mertz, tony and pricey, but smart, too. Both of them were the godchildren of a local boy named Mark Mercer, who had made sure that the Beef State no longer lacked places to consume foie gras poached in Sauternes or mallard breasts bedecked with a medley of fig, green bean, arugula, orange and pattypan squash.

And in Des Moines, I located another true believer at Bistro Montage. Enosh Kelly, the chef-owner at this small, intense neighborhood restaurant, was a national figure in his field and deserved the reputation he was getting, with nominations for best chef in the Midwest at the 2009 Beard Awards and kudos from other bellwethers.

There were plenty of tricky first courses on his menu—a *salade niçoise* with "house-canned" ahi tuna and Foxhollow quail eggs with a caper, egg and truffle vinaigrette, for example. But I was in a locavore mood and opted for the farmers' market tomato salad, a mosaic of heirloom tomatoes as many-colored as Joseph's coat, dotted with tangy white flecks of local goat cheese set atop some mild arugula.

From this celebration of the Iowa terroir, I moved on to "liver and onions," a clever turn on the homely dish that usually bears that name. Kelly's liver—an organic local calf's liver, of course—was crisp on the outside, very pink within, cut in triangles and placed on a circular thin cake of grated potato, the great Swiss dish *rösti*. And Kelly didn't forget the onions. They were the caramelized solid matter in the dark brown sauce.

Like the other nice midwesterners in the little dining room, I cleaned my plate and ordered dessert. With no fanfare at all, the menu offered *marjolaine*, the trademark dessert of Fernand Point, godfather of all things *nouvelle*. *Marjolaine* is a pastry chef's spectacular, with thin layers of nut-embellished meringue and butter cream. On the way out, I glanced at a shelf of cookbooks, heavy tomes by contemporary world-beaters, including Thomas Keller and Heston Blumenthal. Kelly was keeping the wide world in his sights, from the banks of the Des Moines River.

The best proof that a top chef could land on his feet in the most unpromising, chilly, remote corner of the heartland was a roadhouse named Nokomis, perched on a bluff overlooking the western end of Lake Superior just outside Duluth. Sean Lewis moved up there to raise his children near family and to indulge his passion for hunting and fishing. He opened Nokomis after stints in various Chicago restaurants, including a gig with the gifted and internationally praised chef Jean Joho at the Everest, atop the Chicago Stock Exchange.

I hadn't been in Duluth since I'd passed through on my way to canoe in the Quetico-Superior Wilderness area before college. Now, fifty years later, I was in town to visit a friend serving a long sentence for embezzlement at a nearby federal prison camp. On a sunny day, on the terrace at Nokomis, I felt as if I were sitting on the first-class sundeck of an ocean liner. There was nothing much between me and my walleye po'boy and Longfellow's "shining Big-Sea-Water." Lake Superior is the world's biggest freshwater lake by surface area (Baikal, in Siberia, has more water).

Longfellow called it Gitche Gumee in his Ojibway epic *The Song of Hiawatha;* Nokomis is named for Hiawatha's grandmother ("Daughter of the Moon, Nokomis"), who pitched her wigwam by its shores. Obviously, I told myself, Lewis wants his customers to think about local traditions when they eat here—the Indian legends, French exploration, iron-ore shipping; his menu, while mostly international and modern, featured a few local specialties. He had converted an Atlantic Coast favorite, the crab cake, into a whitefish cake, with a mustard rémoulade, brioche and roasted peppers to surround this peerless lake fish's smoked flavor and tender flesh. He turned out a hand-chopped and very lean elk burger (farmed, of course, and not gamy but, shall we say, of independent spirit compared with ground beef).

The top of the food chain at Nokomis, for me, however, was that walleye sandwich. Walleye is a very big deal hereabouts. It's the state fish; Great Lakes fishermen net them in the millions, and restaurants of every sort serve them in every form, from beer-battered to blackened. The perfectly broiled piece of walleye I ate exemplified what cookbooks call "fleshy white fish." Moist, sweet-tasting and fleshy, this was supreme fish, in a truly superior setting.

If Nokomis showed the spread of advanced ideas in their simplest form at the farthest possible distance from the source, other heartland restaurants were barely less sophisticated than Per Se or San Francisco's molecular-gastronomic Coi, and much closer to the source of their food.

Josh Adams brought the modernist, locavore gospel from Alinea to bleak Peoria, his hometown. From the open kitchen of June, he could draw on several nearby central Illinois farms, including an eighty-acre certified-organic operation contracted exclusively to supply him.

For someone like me who remembered the gastronomic desert that the heartland had been fifty years before Josh Adams smoked shiitake mushrooms in coffee or turned out eerily tender Muscovy duck breasts by sous vide slow cooking, this return of educated chefs to the rural terroirs of their birth was immensely gratifying. But June was more than a culmination of trends that had started elsewhere. It combined the broad and established locavore-organic-healthy theology spawned by a motley crew of nutritionally zealous aesthetes descended from such diverse gurus as Adelle Davis, Alice Waters, Euell Gibbons and Michael Pollan, with the technical assistance of the transcendental, prestidigitational Mr. Wizards of El Bulli, the Fat Duck and Momofuku Ko. At June, these two opposites—the perfectly pure and homegrown versus the completely unnatural—could coexist in perilous balance on the smallest of carbon footprints.

But in the hurly-burly of the global food scene, the 365-day-a-year Olympics of Michelin stardom and San Pellegrino rankings for the world's fifty greatest restaurants, there was no perilous balance between purity of ingredients and the inventive genius of the chef. In this arena, the genius chefs triumphed.

Innovation, cheekiness toward tradition—these were the same traits that got the nouvelle cuisine chefs of the 1970s worldwide acclaim. But Guérard and Bocuse and the Troisgros had all built on culinary tradition. The molecular gastronomers had raced beyond them with advanced machinery and food chemistry, much of it borrowed from the kitchens of the commercial food industry. With these techniques, they literally reinvented food, re-formed it.

Led at first by Ferran Adrià at El Bulli, they attracted record numbers of requests for reservations.* In every year before 2010, when Ferran Adrià announced that he would close El Bulli, at the peak of its celebrity, on July 30, 2011, it was in the top three of the San Pellegrino list published in the United Kingdom's *Restaurant* magazine. From 2006 through 2009, El Bulli led the list, followed by the Fat Duck. Despite the fame and popularity, El Bulli, according to Adrià, did not turn a profit. Open only half the year, with a chef in the kitchen for every diner, it was an extravagant experiment.

It would be easy to dismiss all this as a sign of the basic vulgarity of the glamorous, chef-worshipping, trendy top end of the restaurant scene. It is pretty clear that the selection system behind the list is a dodgy affair: the writers and bons viveurs who do the voting are not even required to submit proof that they have actually eaten in any restaurant. Some voters have admitted publicly that they form blocs to get their pals or neighbors chosen. It's important, however, to remember that the list has not created the reputations of its favorites but merely latched onto the coattails of serious chefs already renowned in the gossipy world of food pros and dedicated epicures.

In 1999, three years before *Restaurant* magazine started the San Pellegrino list, the American wine and food journalist Jacqueline Friedrich proposed an article for my page at the *Journal* about a radical restaurant in an isolated bay in rural Catalonia. She had been hearing great things about it in Paris, where she was based. I gave her the assignment. She ate at El Bulli twice, interviewed Adrià, and wrote a highly favorable piece. She said just about everything worth saying about Adrià and the movement he had launched, in 1,241 words. The food was "startling." Major chefs like Joël Robuchon were making pilgrimages over the scary road

---

* According to the restaurant, two million people applied by e-mail for reservations at El Bulli on the first day bookings were accepted for 2009.

from Rosas and coming back with ecstatic reports. Friedrich saw that the tasting menu of more than twenty small plates was a crucial innovation (which would go a long way toward ending the traditional appetizer, main course, dessert format in hundreds of other restaurants).

Adrià, she wrote, was upending basic ideas about salty and sweet combinations; his almond ice cream was studded with garlic slivers and splashed with oil and vinegar. There were deconstructions of Catalan regional dishes: bread rubbed with tomato and garlic, then drizzled with olive oil (*pa amb tomàquet*) and turned into "grape-sized pellets of crisp pizza dough, which, when bitten into, release gushes of olive oil." And the tomato? It was on the side as a scoop of sorbet.

These were the conventional items. Then came the notorious *espumas*, the foams. Adrià got a lot of bad press for these seaweed-gel-thickened essences sprayed out of seltzer siphons. But Friedrich saw that this wasn't a gimmick and got Adrià to explain why he did it: "Typically you mount a mousse with cream. But that dilutes its flavor. If you mount raspberries with cream, you get the flavor of raspberries and cream. I wanted just the raspberries. Nothing else. I want the pure flavor of the froth you find on top of freshly squeezed orange juice."

Friedrich, like so many who followed her to El Bulli, got the point of the wilder dishes, the aesthetic joy and surprise that science and imagination could produce. For instance, there was the soup made of frozen peas fresh from the freezer and hot mineral water; it was served in a glass and drunk in one long slurp, during which it changed from hot to cold. She praised the improbable but thrillingly successful, surreal combinations, such as the strip of phyllo dough "topped with diced pineapple" and white truffle shavings and basil and fresh almonds.

I went to El Bulli myself first in February 2001, when it was closed for its long winter nap. The lonely, twisting drive has often been described. Adrià himself has said it is an essential part of the El Bulli experience, making a meal there the reward at the end of a difficult journey that begins with the struggle for a reservation. There is also the setting, a cliff overlooking a lost cove. (Well, not entirely lost. At the water's edge is a modest retirement community.)

I made the trip again the next year. El Bulli's twentieth anniversary seemed like a good time to assess the achievement of the place, because the menu featured dishes from all the past years. There were twenty-six courses, mostly small and surreal, beautiful creations unlike anything my wife or I had ever eaten before. Starting with an intense mojito pumped out of a siphon, we moved on to little white paper cones filled with fine white powder. Before the waiter had a chance to say what it was, Johanna knocked hers back and aspirated enough of the pulverized popcorn to precipitate a choking fit. She recovered in time to join me in the "snack" courses, among which were rose-petal tempura, brilliant red orbs en brochette (a melon ball and a cherry tomato), a crunchy object made out of quail egg, and an anise-flavored consommé siphoned into a beer mug and looking quite a bit like a dark ale with a two-inch head.

There was much, much more in which science played a transforming role, with gels and slow-cooking, dehydration, colloidal trickery—all the magic of so-called molecular gastronomy harnessed to intensify and concentrate the diner's notions and experience of food.

Every one of those dishes and hundreds of others served at El Bulli between its relatively conservative beginnings in 1983 to the end of the 2004 season were meticulously recorded in four very heavy and expensive tomes. Each dish appears in a color photograph and is cross-indexed and pigeonholed as to its culinary parameters. Each volume has a fold out graphic chart and a CD with recipes for every dish, clear but impractical for the home cook without access to sea cucumbers or the wild mushroom known in Catalan as *rossinyol*, not to mention such arcane and expensive kitchen tools as sous vide baths, Anti-Griddles, and specialty chemicals, *and* the will to take on the elaborate tasks that forty-some sous-chefs performed in the very large open kitchen at El Bulli.

Unlike his spiritual forefathers in the nouvelle cuisine revolution, Adrià was determined to tell the world everything, all his discoveries, his theories. So you don't need me to deconstruct his deconstructions. You do have to be willing to spend several hundred dollars on his books and be able to read them in Spanish or Catalan, but the effort will definitely expand your horizons across many parameters. For example, you will learn that *palomitas* is Spanish for "popcorn" and *cucurucho* refers to those paper cones that nearly flattened my wife. And the combination of pictures, recipes and pontification will convince you almost as much as living through an actual meal at El Bulli that it was a place that took a giant step forward in what one might still call cooking.

"Deconstruction" was not a word the man used lightly. He took ingredients and dismantled them, repurposed them and then made them look like normal food, especially normal Spanish food. I'm thinking right now about his *morcilla*, blood pudding, which is a dish as common in Spain as hot dogs are here. *Morcilla*, the really common version I first ordered by mistake way past my bedtime in Burgos in 1963, looks, when sliced, like a black blini with white maggots in it. Adrià fashioned faux-*morcilla* slices that looked just like the real thing with rice and squid ink.

Now, there's nothing outré about rice and squid ink. It is, itself, a well known combination of flavors around the Mediterranean. So if you grew up on *morcilla* as well as rice tinged black with squid ink, you would love biting into this dish thinking it's blood sausage and then having your taste memory tell you it's rice with squid ink. This is, however, a very different kind of high-level fun from the gentle and buried ironies of nouvelle cuisine. Think about it. Calling thin-cut salmon an escalope, as the Troigros brothers did, merely suggested that those pieces of salmon were "like" veal scaloppine. The menu said right out that you'd be getting salmon, and if you were tipsy from aperitifs or not paying attention, you might have missed the point of the metaphoric labeling, but that wouldn't have mattered, since the salmon, in its sorrel sauce, was a very excellent dish by any name.

Adrià wasn't playing that kind of subtle game. He was flaunting his tricks. Anyone who had ever eaten *morcilla* knew at first bite, if not at first sight, this one was a (brilliant) fabrication. Figuring out what it really was was like a second punch line that just about any Spaniard got the point of.

A lot of the dishes at El Bulli were harder to figure out than the *morcilla*. The science wasn't common knowledge for any normal diner, but the intense flavors of those desiccated ingredients—say, the spices and herbs that surrounded the cauliflower turned into couscous—helped justify the magic show. Adrià's food was full of major flavors, many of them not easily identifiable, because he had combined ingredients rarely, or never before, so conjoined. I am thinking of the smoked eel accompanied by ravioli filled with a mixture of pineapple and fennel he invented in 1998.

In one of many similar anecdotes in his El Bulli almanacs about the origins of his dishes, Adrià writes:

A visit to a Japanese restaurant inspired us to create a dish with smoked eel. But we needed to come up with an accompaniment for it that would balance the fattiness of the eel [*desengrasante*]. And although we were in the middle of a period of creating new hot raviolis, we thought that the right thing for this [hot] dish was a cold ravioli. Remembering the slices of pineapple in the pineapple soup with candied fennel and star anise flan of 1994, we decided to make a ravioli with the same ingredients. The filling, as in the earlier dessert, would be the fennel, in this case made into a jelly.*

To make fennel jelly, Adrià cooks thin slices and leaves them in boiling water until soft, then purees them in a blender and forces the puree through a fine strainer. Then he mixes the strained fennel with gelatin and spreads a thin layer of it in a pan and refrigerates the mixture until it gels and can be cut into three-quarter-inch squares.

It is also worth mentioning the delicate cooking of the eel, its meat-stock-based orange sauce and its garnishes (fried strips of eel skin, ground star anise and grated orange peel), as well as explaining that the ravioli skins were very thin squares of pineapple. All that is clearly spelled out in the recipe on the CD.

In the pell-mell of twenty-six courses, it was a definite challenge to appreciate all of these remarkable details, even with the helpful commentary of the waitstaff (three individuals, if I recall correctly). But it was always clear that each dish was intricate, unprecedented and extremely delicious, if sometimes baffling without exegesis.

As a critic for the *Journal*, I ate in most of the other leading modernist restaurants—the ones I've mentioned, the Fat Duck in Bray-on-Thames (U.K.), Alinea in Chicago, both of Thomas Keller's flagship restaurants, and Momofuku Ko and WD-50 in New York—as well as several others in Spain. They are adventurous places with a commitment to use science to reinvent dining,

* Translation mine.

culinary laboratories that won the feverish allegiance of millions of well-heeled diners around the world for their use of advanced technology in the service of culinary spectacle. They are also the targets of mockery for their more extreme dishes, foams, burning hay, atomized aromas.

I'm biting my tongue to avoid the label the modernists have come to hate: molecular gastronomy. It was coined to describe a workshop bringing together chefs and scientists back in 1992, by the physicist Nicholas Kurti, whom I had met at the Oxford Symposium on Food and Cookery. But the term quickly caused more confusion than it was worth, almost inviting people to dismiss its practitioners as shallow stuntmen with no respect for the past or for fundamental culinary values.

Adrià, Heston Blumenthal of the Fat Duck and Keller did their best to dispel public misunderstanding with a manifesto released at the end of 2006. "We do not pursue novelty for its own sake," they wrote. "We may use modern thickeners, sugar substitutes, enzymes, liquid nitrogen, sous-vide, dehydration and other non-traditional means, but these do not define our cooking. They are a few of the many tools that we are fortunate to have available as we strive to make delicious and stimulating dishes."*

Blumenthal, a sometime Oxford symposiast, has consulted regularly with scientists, yet he deliberately creates an atmosphere of playful experimentation in his intimate three-star Michelin restaurant in a village very close to London's Heathrow Airport. His preoccupation with the simple foods of his British childhood and with the tastes of everyday life have inspired some of his most advanced and arresting dishes.

Anglo-French amity took a slow glide forward when Blumenthal combined snails and oatmeal, with all the traditional ingredi-

---

* Quoted in *The Big Fat Duck Cookbook*, by Heston Blumenthal (London: Bloomsbury, 2008), page 127.

ents of classic *escargots de Bourgogne:* garlic, butter and parsley, lots of parsley, for a very green presentation of snails on an oat risotto with the texture of rice pudding.

While seeking the perfect palate cleanser to begin a meal, Blumenthal started with toothpaste and ended up with a masterpiece of scientific manipulation of flavors that really did cleanse the palate and wake up the diner's taste buds. On my visit to the restaurant in 2009, the famous nitro-poached green tea and lime mousse was prepared in front of me. The waiter squeezed out some of the toothpaste-resembling mousse into the extreme cold of liquid nitrogen, which "cooked" it into a sort of meringue. It was then spattered with green tea dust and sprayed with lime essence from an atomizer. The mousse, warmed by the mouth in one gulp, seemed to disappear, leaving a pure, mildly acidic and tannic freshness. I was very pleasantly surprised and ready to eat "real" food.

One of the next dishes served was the "sound of the sea" that I'd first tried (and heard) when Blumenthal served it at Charlie Trotter's twentieth-anniversary dinner in Chicago.* The main course that followed helped me overcome a bad feeling about licorice lingering from childhood: salmon sheathed in a black licorice gel with artichoke, vanilla mayonnaise and an elite olive oil.

It turns out that Blumenthal didn't start out liking licorice much, either. As he describes it in a commentary on a similar recipe in his sprightly and very grand *The Big Fat Duck Cookbook*, he was led to use licorice because he had learned that it shared an enzyme with asparagus and he thought that the extreme sweetness of the licorice and the bitterness of the asparagus might balance each other out. At the same time, he was experimenting with gellan, a gelling medium. Mixing it with licorice, he came up with a perfect coating for a strong fish. The shiny black licorice played

* See page 186.

TASTING MENU AND WINE

NITRO-POACHED GREEN TEA AND LIME MOUSSE (2001)
ORANGE AND BEETROOT JELLY
OYSTER, PASSION FRUIT JELLY, LAVENDER
POMMERY GRAIN MUSTARD ICE CREAM, RED CABBAGE GAZPACHO
JELLY OF QUAIL, LANGOUSTINE CREAM, PARFAIT OF FOIE GRAS
OAK MOSS AND TRUFFLE TOAST
(Homage to Alain Chapel)

2007 RIESLING KABINETT, JOH. JOS. PRÜM, MOSEL

(GERMANY)

SNAIL PORRIDGE
Jabugo Ham, Shaved Fennel

2007 CHATEAUNEUF DU PAPE, DOMAINE DE BEAURENARD

(FRANCE)

ROAST FOIE GRAS "BENZALDEHYDE"
Almond Fluid Gel, Cherry and Chamomile

2004 PINOT GRIS, ROLLY GASSMANN, ALSACE

(FRANCE)

"SOUND OF THE SEA"
GINJO SAKE DEWAZAKURA, YAMAGATA

(JAPAN)

SALMON POACHED IN LIQUORICE GEL
Artichoke, Vanilla Mayonnaise and "Manni" Olive Oil

2001 QUINTA DA LEDA, CASA FERREIRINHA, DOURO VALLEY

(PORTUGAL)

BALLOTINE OF ANJOU PIGEON
Black Pudding "Made to Order", Pickling Brine and Spiced Juices

2005 Tokara, Merlot/Cabernet Sauvignon/Petit Verdot, Stellenbosch
(South Africa)

HOT AND ICED TEA (2005)

MRS MARSHALL'S MARGARET CORNET

PINE SHERBET FOUNTAIN
(PRE-HIT)

MANGO AND DOUGLAS FIR PUREE
Bavarois of Lychee and Mango, Blackcurrant Sorbet

2005 Breganze Torcolato, Maculan, Veneto
(Italy)

PARSNIP CEREAL

NITRO-SCRAMBLED EGG AND BACON ICE CREAM (2006)
Pain Perdu and Tea Jelly

2006 Jurançon, Uroulat, Charles Hours, South West
(France)

PETITS FOURS
Carrot and Orange Lolly, Mandarin Aerated Chocolate

Apple Pie Caramel "Edible Wrapper", Violet Tartlet

At the Fat Duck, west of London, in 2009, I dived into Heston Blumenthal's literal re-creation, both on a plate and in sound piped through an iPod Shuffle, of a littoral teeming with wonderful fishy and crustacean things to eat.

beautifully against the fatty taste of the salmon. And the gel stayed solid inside an evacuated plastic bag while the salmon poached for twenty-five minutes at the very low temperature of 108 degrees F. The black-giving-way-to-orange contrast as you cut into the fish added an element of circus dash.

I read this explanation in *The Big Fat Duck Cookbook* after I had eaten the dish. Blumenthal's account of the way he stumbled toward its final conception enhanced my appreciation of what I'd eaten. And the recipe that followed let me see exactly how he'd brought it off. This kind of clarity and transparency is not just an accidental habit of the modernist chefs. It is a commitment they share that there will be no more chef's secrets on their watch.

This is admirable, and practical. It leaves no room for the kind of misinterpretation that inevitably built up around the tight-lipped and subtle masters of nouvelle cuisine. But it does still leave open a major esthetic question.

Since modernist cuisine depends so heavily on surprise and theatricality, will a second visit to these restaurants be as exciting as the first? Once you know that the mousse will vanish in your mouth and that the black fish is really orange inside, will you still want to speed-dial the Fat Duck two months in advance to snag one of the restaurant's forty seats, and fly in for the day from Melbourne for the occasion? When you know how the magician cuts the lady in half, do you want to see him do it a second time?

Vladimir Nabokov saw this as a central issue for readers of fiction. He made his students at Cornell read all the assigned novels in his course twice so that the second time around they would be able to look beyond the sentimental seductions of the plot to enjoy, say, Jane Austen for her art. Of course, a novel has a fixed text and a restaurant can and usually does change its menu over time. But the question remains: Will the attraction of culinary contrivance and coups de théâtre wear off? Will the excitement of modernist food pale?

For most people, there will be no second chance or even a first, given the difficulty of getting a seat at these places and their high cost. But in the long haul, for the gastronome committed to dining at the cutting edge, it does matter if a cooking style built on magic and chemical disguise, on the novelty of improbable mixtures of ingredients and violations of traditional taste affinities, can weather familiarity.

Science may offer an answer. What may start as dramatic novelty in the laboratory can turn into an indispensable feature of normal life. The original laser was once the stuff of science fiction, but lasers now read DVDs in millions of households.

Something similar has already occurred in the restaurant world. Sous vide cooking, which was nearly outlawed as a health risk by clueless New York City health inspectors, is now a regular fact of life in utterly routine restaurants with no flash to them. Meanwhile, the best of the cutting-edge modernists continue to develop. That is their gift. They build on what they've learned. But even a talented modernist chef can end up making you yawn. I was dazzled the first time I ate at Grant Achatz's Alinea. The second time, his act seemed shallow. a bevy of stunts disguising a lot of dishes of routine flavor.

This may explain why he has opened a second restaurant, called Next, that will remake not only its menu but its entire concept every quarter, doing pastiches and reenactments of food from past eras, exotic venues and other men's restaurants. Food as a postmodern variety show.

At the same time, the era of the molecular modernists may already have peaked. El Bulli is closed, and the top spot in the San Pellegrino ratings for 2011 was won by a restaurant known for prescientific foraging. Noma, in Copenhagen, built its menu around seaweed and other foodstuffs gathered from Scandinavian shores and forests.

Despite its militantly Nordic primitivism, Noma was a direct descendant of culinary modernism, not a reaction against it. René Redzepi, a Danish citizen whose father is Albanian-Macedonian, worked at El Bulli before founding Noma in an old salt shed on a bleak pier on the Copenhagen waterfront. He also worked for Thomas Keller at the French Laundry, and several members of his staff, when I had lunch there in February 2012, had come from the kitchen of Keller's Per Se, in New York. And the food, while rigorously sourced from its region, almost pedantically seasonal (including items picked fresh in warmer weather and then pickled or salted for the winter), and austerely presented, could not have existed without the deconstructive irony of nouvelle cuisine or modernism's experiments in transforming edible raw materials into shapes and textures unknown in nature.

Redzepi's spectacular success, which has inspired a wave of imitation in Copenhagen and put Denmark on the world culinary map for the first time in its history (Danish pastry is the exception that proves the rule), made Noma the leading current example of the international nature of elite dining.

Ecstatic notices in the foreign press—especially the top rating in London's *Restaurant* magazine's annual fifty-best restaurant poll—were followed by reverberations in food blogs and a worldwide assault from foodies competing by e-mail for one of the fifteen tables.

Before I went there for lunch on Valentine's Day, I had read Redzepi's manifesto at the front of *Noma: Time and Place in Nordic Cuisine*.* So I knew not to expect luxury ingredients such as foie gras or the meat-based sauces typical of French haute cuisine. Other trappings of the Michelin star circuit would be missing, too. So it didn't surprise me that there were no tablecloths and that the

* London: Phaidon, 2010.

plates were a jumble of plain old things instead of the hand-painted Royal Copenhagen favored in many other leading Copenhagen eating places. And it wasn't a total shock to discover that the food was often served to us by the chefs.

This is a growing trend in smallish avant-garde restaurants with the ambition to democratize the dining experience, to take it further away from the aristocratic food service of the past, and to increase the intimacy of the meal, while demystifying the cooking by promoting dialogue between chefs and customers. Young chefs, in particular at Schwa in Chicago and Momofuku Ko in New York, have favored this approach. And René Redzepi is a young chef. He was only twenty-five when Noma opened its doors in 2004.

The starkness of the foraged subarctic and arctic ingredients was part of the legend that preceded Noma's twenty-four-course lunch. And I fully expected that those mosses and seaweeds, fermented vegetables and strange fish pulled from icy waters would electrify my palate. How many times had I now read reviews bordering on delirium, so many of which ended up with the critic declaring that this had been the "best meal of my life"?

So I thought that, basically, the dishes would sound bizarre but taste great. And this turned out to be true. I was not prepared, however, to find that the presentation of the food, often in simulations of forest floors or tidal pools, was, although deliberately austere compared to the eye-popping techno–trompe l'oeil at El Bulli, Alinea or the Fat Duck, every bit as theatrical, metamorphic and even sometimes comic and irreverent toward local tradition as its more overtly showy and transgressive predecessors'.

This was true right from the first of the fourteen small-plate courses, which were mostly finger food, and which we were encouraged to wash down with a house microbrew based on birch sap. The very first course looked like some kind of Scandinavian ikebana, a faux-haphazard arrangement of juniper sprigs and woody

Malt flatbread and juniper
Moss and cep
Crispy pork skin and black currant
Blue mussel and celery
Dried carrot and sorrel
Caramelized milk and cod liver
Cookies and cheese, rocket and stems
Rye, chicken skin and peas
Potato and chicken liver
Veal fibres and seaweed
Pickled and smoked quails egg
Radish, soil and grass
Herb toast and smoked cod roe
Æbleskiver and muikku

Lunch at Noma on Valentine's Day 2012 was a love feast of foraged, pickled, smoked ingredients plucked from Nordic woods and lakesides, but
then transformed by René Redzepi's decidedly weird imagination into
mini-landscapes that fooled the eye into thinking the chef-waiters at
Copenhagen's celebrated restaurant were serving our table a plate of coral

Lunch 14th of February 2012

Squid and unripe sloe berry
White currant and pine

Dried scallops and beech nuts
Biodynamic grains and watercress

Oysters from Limfjorden

Chestnut and bleak roe
Walnut and rye

Langoustine and söl
Rye and sea

Celeriac and truffle

Pickled vegetables and bone marrow
Browned butter and parsley

Wild duck and beets
Beech and malt

Pear tree!

Potato and plums

anemones (really thin-sliced cylinders of vinegar-steeped vegetables) or marrow bones (caramel). This mad synthesis of nature and technique took place at a pier on an icebound canal, really bleak. So was the roe we ate, which came from a local fish, the bleak. No joke.

twigs, except that the twigs were in fact branching sticks of malty flatbread.

Next came a terra-cotta plate full of reindeer moss, which looked as if it had been dug up outside Valhalla, except that someone clever had fried it a bit so that it crunched, while your palate discovered that the missing mushroom listed on the menu was cèpe powder. Dried carrot sticks were still orange but had taken on the chewy texture and sweetness of licorice, without losing their essential carrothood.

Danes, no doubt, got a special frisson from the lovely arching fried pork rinds covered with a thin layer of black currant leather. This was supposed to remind you of some folkloric local snack made from pork cracklings. It was remarkable enough in its audacious pairing of two "skins," fatty pork and sheets of purplish acidic fruit.

A bit later came a pan-Nordic send-up of *aebleskiver* and *muikku*, Danish balls of pancake dough and small smoked Finnish fish, respectively. The fish appeared to have swum partway through the spheres, like those arrows on children's hats that look as if they had pierced their wearers' tiny heads. Grotesque, yes, but an entirely delicious interpenetration of a traditional Christmas goodie by pesky minnows.

The slightly more imposing ten "main" courses were often constructed as fanciful "habitats," suggesting locales where their ingredients could have been foraged. Intricately treated oysters had been reshelled and then arrayed on pebbles. Thinly sliced dried scallops perched on watercress and squid ink, but the primitive wheat grains intermixed with them did not fit in this seascape. The chef's palate must have trumped his eco-aesthetic here, sensing that a touch of prehistoric starch—emmer and spelt—would stand up nicely to the intense, brittle scallops.

I'd say the same about the unforgettable combination of thin-sliced raw chestnuts and pink roe from the bleak, a local fish. The forest-fresh young chestnut, was, by itself, uningratiatingly woody and astringent. But the delicate buttery roe needed just this gruff, crunchy pairing to match its rich and sea-strong flavor and smoothness. So, for me, the logic of the dish was, once again, in the mouth, not in some simulated landscape.

Certainly, you could not imagine any real-world habitat, except perhaps a coral reef, that would ever have been home to the "signature" platter of seven vegetables pickled in seven different vinegars. Some painstaking apprentice had cut those vegetables paper-thin and rolled the resulting multicolored membranes into cylinders. On the plate, these tubes loomed brightly among pale slices of poached bone marrow, which was a rare intrusion of meatiness (but not muscle meat) into Noma's almost meatless universe. Each tube had its own taste and color in a surreal rainbow that reminded me of scenes nature offers the scuba diver: polyps and sea anemones standing up on the ocean floor.

It was strange and rich. And, some would say, only for the rich. But Noma's popularity produced a sort of democracy of the well-heeled. Like all of the great meals now being served around the world in cutting-edge restaurants, lunch (or dinner) at Noma was available only to a tiny fraction of the potential audience of food lovers able and willing to make a special trip to Copenhagen and pay almost $300 (not including beverage) for their four-hour marathon of invention.

The price was high, sure, but compared to what? A mediocre suit? Teenagers find that much money for tickets to hip-hop concerts.

If I were Redzepi or Heston Blumenthal, I'd be more concerned about the visceral distaste their food, or the written accounts of it, have provoked among people who have never adjusted to any of the changes that have challenged traditional food service at every level of expense and sophistication since the 1960s. Modernist cuisine is only the latest convolution and the one furthest from home cooking. Yet, despite the paranoia of some food-world paleoconservatives, it does not threaten the survival of old-fashioned recipes or of the family life that has sustained them for centuries. The family meal owes its decline to forces far greater than Thomas Keller, Wylie Dufresne and all the artist-chefs to have plated a dish since Fernand Point. Canapés cunningly composed with crackling from hand-raised heritage hogs and leather confected from handpicked black currants will never replace pot roast on the dinner tables of the 99 percent. Packaged food has already done that.

But the dazzling revolution I have witnessed in the food world since 1971 is nevertheless a potent force, more potent across the breadth of most modern societies than the avant-garde achievements of any other modern art. I am talking here about the upgrading of food at all levels of expense and connoisseurship, from the arcane temples of culinary modernism to the airport sandwich shop to the chain supermarket to the average home kitchen. The real revolution everyone above the poverty line enjoys today is a revolution of knowledge and technology, of a food supply of unprecedented variety and ameliorated quality, of a global reach and xenophilia that far surpass the efforts of diplomats and NGOs to bring us all together at one political table.

We owe this unprecedented cornucopia to the success of well-informed chefs and cookbook authors, of food critics and health-food advocates—an elite of tastemakers and providers of examples of the good gastronomic life. It all started with food-minded travelers, with writers propounding an alternative to the cuisine of home economists in books filled with authentic recipes from the great traditional cuisines, with chefs who fanned out around the world cooking those same dishes and then improvised on them in their own spirit. The gospel spread and it converted millions, all newly alert to a standard of quality unknown or unavailable fifty years ago in the most prosperous and best-educated nations in history.

There is a dark side to this. Obesity is the hobgoblin that stalks a food-mad culture. Fast food, and its effect on our health, mocks our claims of sophistication and refinement. But there really has been a radical growth of good taste, now firmly entrenched in the homes of Food Network watchers and in the malls where they shop.

After returning from Noma, I made a tour of the supermarket nearest to my home in the semirural Hudson Valley eighty miles north of New York City. Alongside the aisles of staples and soaps and pet food were hundreds of specialty items beyond the dreams of any American shopper, even in New York City, when I started out there in 1967. In those days, if you wanted clarified butter, you followed Julia's directions and made it yourself, painstakingly. Now I can buy the Indian version of it, ghee, prepared in Sedalia, Colorado.

My supermarket also offers me dozens of filled pastas, ready-to-bake pizza dough, and several kinds of basmati rice (some of it domestically grown). In addition to generic bread crumbs, I can now purchase more delicate Japanese panko. The meat department carries pancetta, the unsmoked bacon that was once a crucial barrier to the authentic preparation of Italian classic dishes outside Italy. At the end of the aisle is a fish department, with wild-caught salmon and live lobsters in tanks.

There are also several aisles of products aimed at the health-minded customer, who formerly had to buy dreary stuff in special shops selling wilted kale. Now my supermarket lets me stay pure while indulging in chipotle sweet potato soup. I can still remember when Manhattan's most highly regarded Mexican restaurant listed chipotle peppers on its menu but never actually had them available.

Back then we trekked to the Arab enclave on Atlantic Avenue

in South Brooklyn to buy hummus, which has now been totally naturalized. I lost count of the different varieties currently for sale ten minutes from my house in exurbia. Prepared and uncooked tabbouleh has also been assimilated by the mass market. As has the crusty French loaf, which I now find baked in my supermarket's in-house bakery with dough shipped in from a central supplier. Elite boutique bakers in the city may do an even better job, but the gap is narrowing.

Once home from the market, I cook with a *batterie de cuisine* that has also improved decisively since 1971. Before then—and even several years later for most people, including me—there were no food processors. If you wanted to chop or puree, you used a knife or struggled to do the job with a blender. If you wanted to beat egg whites, you could go after them either with a balloon whisk or a less-satisfactory motorized mixer. Now the food processor does the heavy-duty work of chopping and pureeing, while immersion blenders (with whisk attachments) have liberated us from the clogging confinement of the blender jar and the wrist fatigue of the balloon whisk.

I will concede that I still make mayonnaise with a hand whisk, because I like the feel of sudden emulsification, when the yolks seize the oil. I also don't think the processor makes that job easier. But on balance, the processor has made a radical difference in my kitchen. As have several other tools and appliances not available when I started cooking.

Life is also easier with a stovetop that puts out nearly four times the heat of my first gas burners. Life is better, too, with a magnetic induction burner that boils water even faster than that powerful stovetop, with vastly less heat leaked into the room. Life will take a great leap forward when I buy a sous vide machine for the price of a full-size power mixer I barely touch anymore or a microwave oven I turn on only to defrost or reheat.

Forty years in food have turned me from a cynic into an opti-mist. In other areas of life, Gresham's law may hold; the bad drives out the good. But in food, the reverse has been overwhelmingly true. Forty years ago in this country, there was no first-rate American cheese, no radicchio, no world-class restaurant, no fresh foie gras, no Sichuan food and no top chef of native birth.

At the beginning of my eighth decade, I take comfort from two great leaps forward in human life. As a passionate reader and writer, I exult in the scientific advances that have given me the computer and the Internet. As a physical creature chained to a wasting body, I look back with pride at the progress we have made in feeding ourselves and rejoice to think of the even better meals that lie ahead.

Acknowledgments

This book itself is an acknowledgment of the many, many people in my life who opened doors and taught me about food and restaurants, who permitted me to write about food and gave me the money to eat it. So I will limit myself here to thanking those whose generosity contributed directly to the work at hand. Jason Epstein steered me enthusiastically away from the laziness of a simple compilation of my restaurant pieces for the *Wall Street Journal* and toward the soul-stretching labor of a memoir, "a real book," he said. (God knows I tried, Jason.) Judith Jones at Knopf agreed that it would be a good idea. She was in a position to know something about my past, since she had presided with wisdom and undeserved fondness over two earlier books, the first of which, *The Saucier's Apprentice*, I proposed to her in 1972, almost at the start of my professional life in food, forty years ago. This time out, I continued to benefit from her care and feeding, which continued after her formal retirement from Knopf in 2011. Then, I also benefited from a new association with Jonathan Segal, a veteran editor at Knopf, who oversaw the meticulous preparation of this book's text for publication with the energy and taste I have known him for since we met at the *New York Times*, more than forty years ago. His assistant, Joey McGarvey, provided invaluable help as well.

Stuart Karle, a great *Journal* pal and a greater attorney, stooped to represent me with Knopf and offered much other wise counsel. Another Dow Jones friend, John Geddes, pointed me to the right people at the *New York Times,* who granted permission for the quotations from my work there and for an extract from a *Times* article by Charlotte Curtis. Tom Weber, yet another *WSJ* mate, made this book's happy ending possible, by hiring me as a born-again restaurant critic at the *Journal*'s Pursuits section in 2006.

Still other friends, John Henry of *Time* and Hendrick Hertzberg of *The New Yorker,* helped me secure rights for illustrations.

Some material in chapter four appeared in a slightly different form in *Natural History;* similarly, some material in chapter five derives from my restaurant columns in *The Wall Street Journal.*

Finally, I thank my wife, Johanna, for sharing meals, sage advice and so much else. *Commensalis, contubernalis, coniunx.*

Index

Illustration Credits

Printed in the United States
by Baker & Taylor Publisher Services